Cooking With Sin

Enjoy this collection of inspiring stories and the recipes that go with them. Each recipe has some kind of alcohol in it: from wine to Irish Cream to home brew. As you make the recipes and sit down at the dinner table, you can share in the moments of each other's lives.

Here's to feeding our bodies and our souls - and having a little fun along the way!

~ Carla

Cooking
Great Recipes Dipped in Alcoho

With Sin

and Wrapped in a Wonderful Story

By Carla Johnson

Edited by Barbara MacLeod and
Kim Stenhouse

First Edition November 2010

www.CookingWithSin.com • www.CarlaJohnson.ca

Edited by Barbara MacLeod & Kim Stenhouse

Design by TruDezign Graphics & Marketing

Photography credits are on pages *10 & 230*

Printed in Canada

ISBN 978-0-9867520-0-1

Dedication

To my Grandmothers,

Elizabeth Voth Nickel Dyck
&
Dorothy Williams Johnson

Two strong, determined women who dedicated themselves to their families and never apologized for their strengths

RECIPES DIPPED IN ALCOHOL AND
IN A WONDERFUL STOR

table of contents

WAYNE ATACK

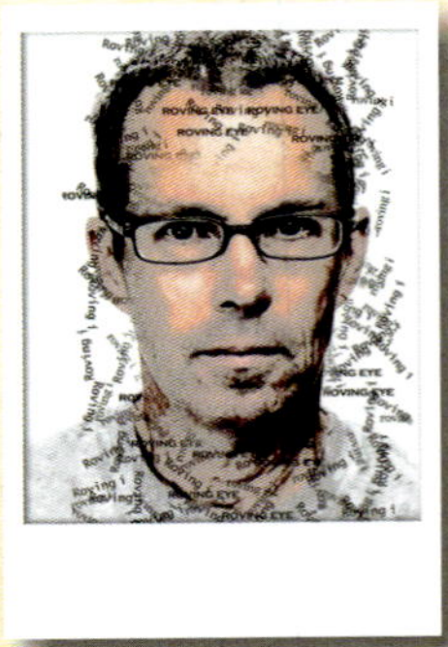

Wayne Atack is the creative genius behind Roving Eye Photographic Services, a Cambridge Ontario based business. Having studied photography at Fanshawe College when traditional processes were still in use, he now embraces the digital medium. A diverse range of experiences has seen him work in locations such as Calgary and Toronto. On the rare occasions when not busy, Wayne can sometimes be found climbing on the Escarpment or engaged in other outdoor activities. Thanks to Carla for the opportunity to contribute to this project - it was an interesting and enjoyable diversion!

Wayne took the outstanding images of "She's a Trooper" Cherries Jubilee recipe and all of the flambé photos throughout the book. His wife Michèle and their two daughters Ariane and Paige had a lot of fun testing the recipe together.

http://www.rovingeye.ca/

AUDREY ROORDA

The moment Audrey Roorda put her camera's viewfinder up to her eye she fell in love with photography. She likes to challenge herself and spent several months sharing a photo a day online. She has also had nice success in the stock photo business. While she works in data management by day, she tends a beautiful garden at home and when she's not hiking or camping, she is very busy volunteering in her community.

Audrey took the gorgeous images of "Poverty Line" German Potato Salad. She especially enjoyed the challenge of finding all the different ways to photograph beer.

Audrey's online name is "Oddrose."

HEATHER JURCZYK

JEFF SHIVELY

Heather Jurczyk and Jeff Shively enjoy cooking and taking pictures for their blog. Together they love to entertain. On their blog they sum it up well, "Good food and good friends and good drink are the cornerstones of our life." They took the delectable photos of "Perfect First Date" Mojito Lamb.

www.HeCooksSheCooks.com

DEREK MARSH

Between working full time and raising two teenage daughters and an energetic son, Derek loves to take time for his photography hobby. He is self-taught and constantly looking for new opportunities to fine tune his skills.

Derek took the photos of "We are Family" Whisky Fondue, some of the photos for "Grandma Started It" Chicken Cacciatore and "Special Delivery" Black Forest Cake.

BRENDA ENGLAND

Brenda England is a wife and mother of three. She enjoys photography, preserving memories through scrapbooking and turning her creations into unique greeting cards.

Brenda shot the beautiful images of "Sin Supper With the Goddesses" Sex in a Pan and "Savoury Scent" Chicken Soup.
http://www.wix.com/BrendaEngland/PinelandCreations

The rest of the food photos were taken by me and I am grateful to the people at Grand Marnier, the Grand Pré Winery in Nova Scotia and The Great Lakes Brewery in Toronto who generously gave me several of their beautiful photos to use freely.

Also, several amazing cooks helped test the recipes. Yes, all the recipes were tested and are wonderful. A great big "Thank you" to my mother-in-law Helen Roorda, my sister-in-law Kate Verhoef, my brother-in-law Austin Roorda and my almost-cousin Tracie Giesbrecht. You showed me new and fun ways to prepare several of the recipes. Another huge thank you to my wonderful friends Sharon Verley and Holly McKenzie Marsh. The three of us spent a really fun day testing 8 of the recipes in one fell swoop. Then we spent the evening on the deck sipping wine and comparing Triple Sec, Cointreau and Grand Marnier. All unforgettable memories!

The most special "Thank you" goes to my family. My husband Steven Roorda supported this project in ways too numerous to mention here, but I can tell you this, he is an amazing partner to walk this journey with. Plus, I took advantage of the fact that his skills in the kitchen truly eclipse mine. Love from the depths of my heart goes to my daughter Daren Roorda who enjoys creating her own signature recipes. She is the reason I challenge myself to be all I can be. It is only when I am pursuing my dreams that I can help her pursue hers.

The wonderful aspect of this book is that it is a collaboration of many people's efforts. I am immensely grateful to each person who shared their heart and their expertise. This book could not have happened without everyone's enthusiastic participation.

"Do you want a collection of brilliant minds or a brilliant collection of minds?" was once asked by Dr. R. Meredith Belbin. Here, in Cooking With Sin, I believe we have both!

INTRODUCTION "THE SPARK"

I once read something that said a life worth living was a life worth writing down. At the time I balked and sneered a bit. "Life is always worth living, but does it have to be written down?" I thought. "If I can't find something to write about, does it mean my life's not worth living?" I was annoyed. But time has a way of making things clearer. As I have gotten better at knowing and embracing myself, I have actually started writing things down. I now write down my ideas, my dreams, my favourite soap-box rants, everything. A few weeks ago that quote came back to mind and I got it.

Many of us think of our lives as being common and ordinary. While it is not always obvious, each of us have lived uncommon extraordinary lives. Sometimes it just takes a scratch and wonderful stories start to pour out.

The phrase "Cooking With Sin" came from my maternal grandmother and her story is the first one I share. Recently I was telling friends this story and it occurred to me that there must be many, many other versions of this same story from many other people and so I began collecting recipe-story combinations from people. I was sweetly surprised by what I found.

You can be certain that any recipe that has a memory attached to it is going to be something special. Some of the stories in this book are about people going against the grain, some are stories of triumph and others are great moments that people treasure for many wonderful reasons.

Cultures and religions around the globe treat alcohol as a "sin" for obviously good reasons. Too much alcohol – like too much of anything – can be a serious problem. We even call the taxes on alcohol a "sin" tax. Yet, even when there are strong forces urging people to follow rules, there is always a rebel or two in the crowd, and they usually have a good story to tell.

I love to eat, I love to share stories and I enjoy a sip of *sin* once in a while. Let me add this. I am not a great cook by any means. In fact, I have a great story about the day I bombed at boiling eggs – they literally exploded! The contributors are the experts and I will let them share their cooking expertise along with something from their hearts.

Food is like a glue. It connects us. My hope is that the stories that come with the recipes make our connections all the richer. When you sit down to eat one of the many dishes, may you feel a bond with the person and the moment in their life they have shared here. We often notice the things that separate us, but we have so much more that connects us and brings us together. That is what I love about the human race!

I *sin*cerely hope you enjoy reading, tasting and sipping every part of this wonderful collection!

~ Carla

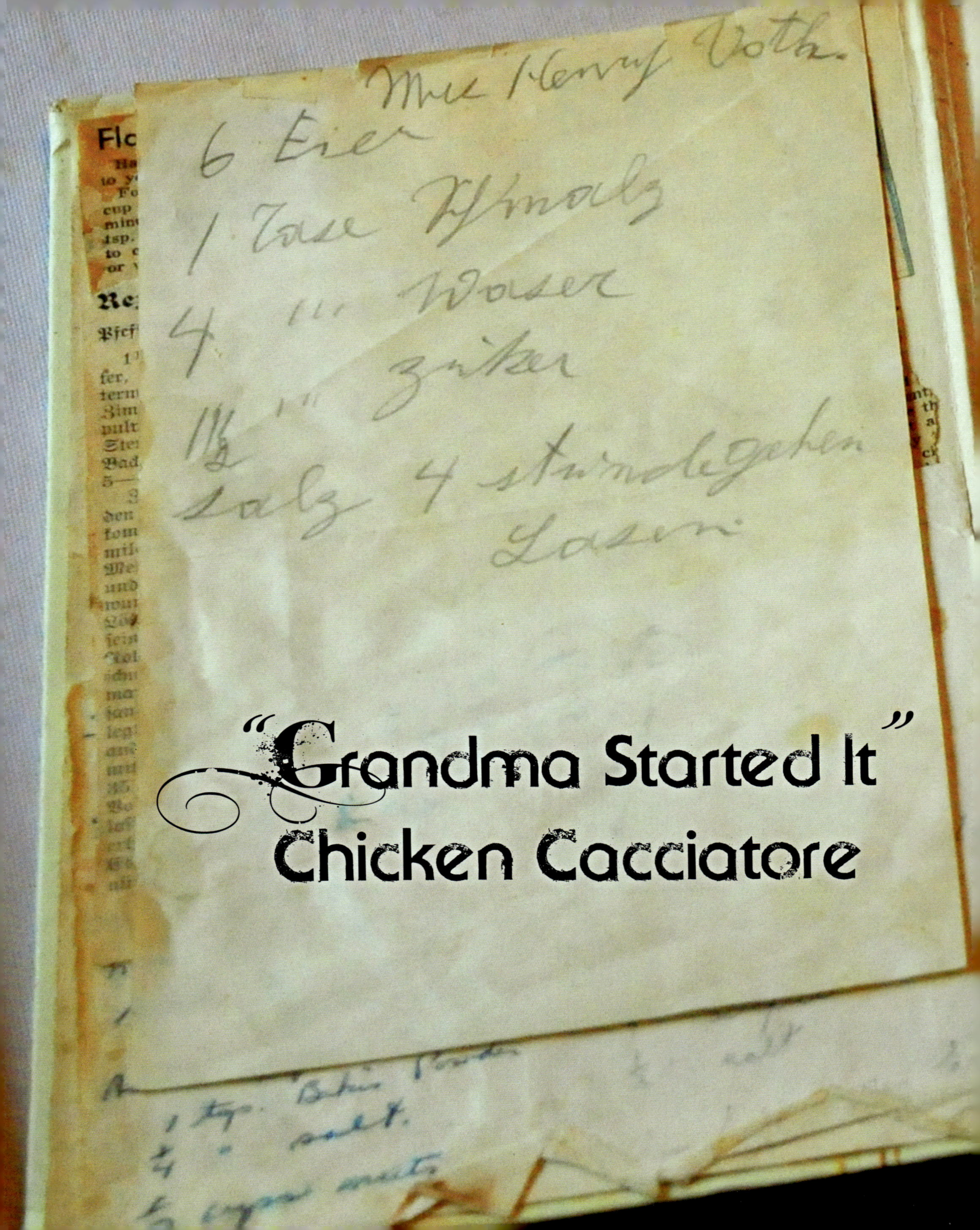

"Grandma Started It" Chicken Cacciatore

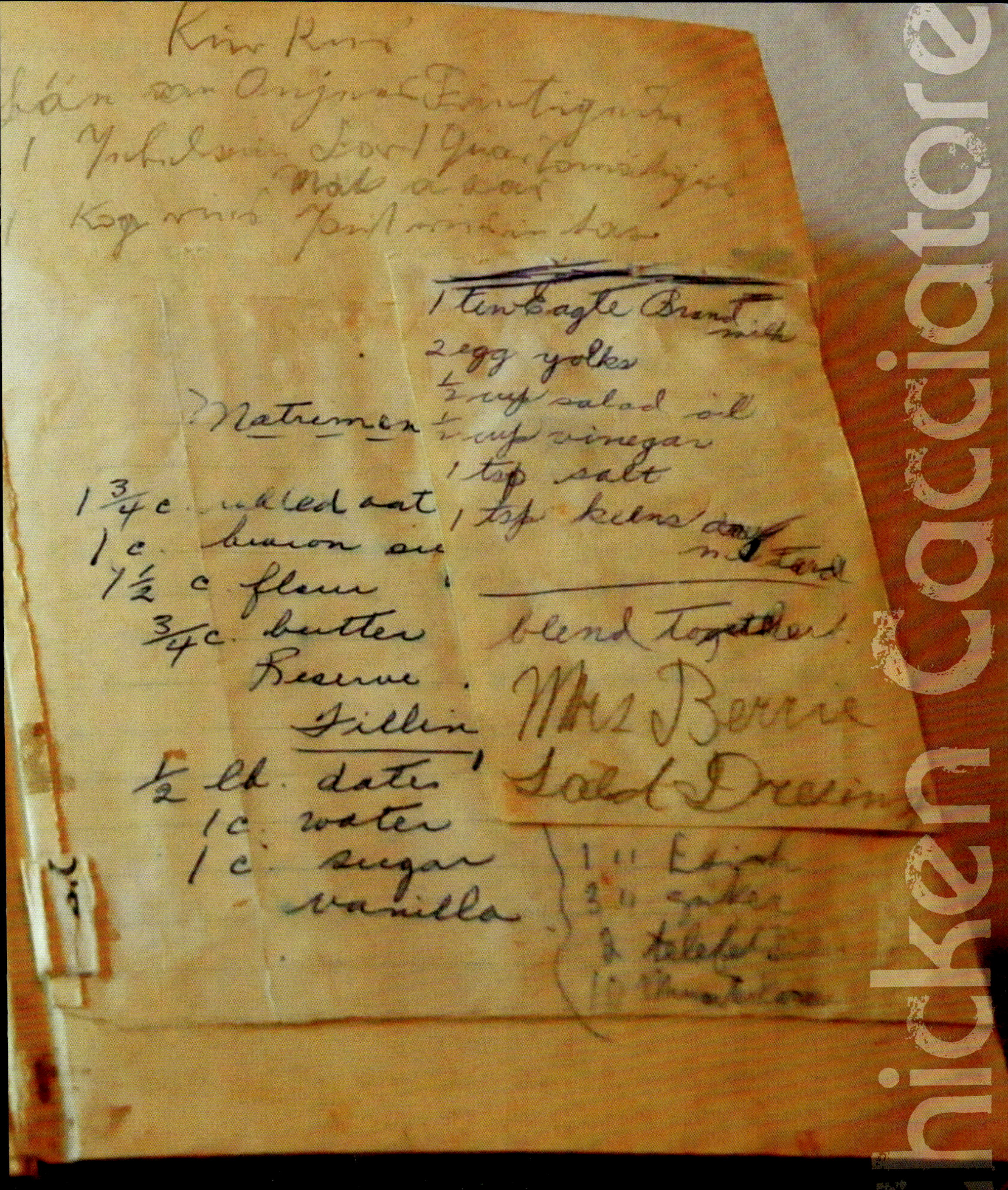
1 tin Eagle Brand milk
2 egg yolks
1/2 cup salad oil
1/2 cup vinegar
1 tsp salt
1 tsp keens dry mustard
blend together.
Mrs Berrie
Salad Dressing
Matrimon
1 3/4 c. rolled oat
1 c. brown su
1 1/2 c flour
3/4 c. butter
Reserve
Fillin
1/2 lb. dates
1 c. water
1 c. sugar
vanilla
hicken cacciatore

The wines that one best remembers are not necessarily the finest that one has ever tasted, and the highest quality may fail to delight so much as some far more humble beverage drunk in more favorable surroundings.
~ H. Warner Allen

My mother, Betty (Nickel) Johnson, was raised in a staunch, devout, Mennonite Brethren home. Her family moved throughout western Canada. She and her five siblings, Jerry, Hank, Alice, Esther and David remain proud and true to their roots, and enjoy sharing tales of the times in which they grew up.

The Mennonite tradition is rooted in simple living and a solid work ethic, so in the 1940s things like nail polish and lipstick made one stand out too much. Smoking, dancing, drinking and playing cards were also taboo. It was often joked that they weren't allowed to have sex because it might lead to dancing.

My maternal grandmother, Elizabeth (Voth) Nickel Dyck (1910-1996), lived the life of a true pioneer. As a teen, she and her family fled the Russian Revolution with only the clothes on their backs. They started off farming in Mexico, then picked up again and travelled to northern Alberta where they settled down to farm the cold prairies. She worked extremely hard her entire life and saw first hand how it paid off for her family. Her priorities were clear. Faith was number one. Work was number two.

When Grandma married my grandfather, John Nickel, and started a family, she was extremely dedicated to making the farm flourish. Her love of work was supported by her enormous stamina. She out-lived two husbands and only slowed down in her mid-eighties just before she passed away. When Grandma first met Steve, my husband, she grabbed his face, nodded approvingly and said, "Good for work."

I grew up in the east. Visits with my western relatives were few and far between. I remember one of Grandma's visits when I was a teen. Mom was making one of my favourite dishes, Chicken Cacciatore, and she liked to add a bit of red wine to her recipe. Please understand, I grew up in a "dry" home. My parents were both devoted non-drinkers. There was never alcohol in our home and I never saw my parents take even a sip of wine until I was in my twenties. On that particular day, mom was hunched cautiously over the stove quickly pouring the red wine into the pan of cooking chicken before Grandma found out. Too late! Grandma came around the corner and abruptly stopped. She had caught my mom "red wine handed" and with her firm voice and Plautdietsch (Low German) accent, she shook her head and scolded, "Cooking with sin, are we?"

It was the first time I ever saw my mom truly defensive. "Oh Mom, the alcohol is cooked off in the pan. It adds a nice flavour. It's fine to eat. Really."

Initially I brushed it off as just another thing my grandmother disapproved of. She had always been very clear about what she liked and didn't like, so her reaction wasn't a surprise, but that particular moment has stuck in my memory. Being a "fly on the wall" witness to Grandma's accusation and Mom's defensive response left a curious imprint on me and ultimately led to the wonderful adventure of this book.

We all happily ate the cacciatore for supper that day and enjoyed every morsel. As the years went by, Grandma mellowed as we all do and became more relaxed about many things. After she passed away, the family was very surprised to find a good stash of liquor in her nursing room cupboard. Way to go, Grandma!

"Grandma Started It" Chicken Cacciatore

Serves 4

Ingredients:

14 fresh button mushrooms
2 tablespoons plus 2 teaspoons olive oil
7-8 chicken thighs
3/4 cup flour
sea salt
pepper
Herbes de provence
1 tablespoon margarine or butter
1 onion, chopped
2 cloves of garlic, chopped
1 large can (796 ml/28 oz) chopped tomatoes
1 can (398 ml/14 oz) chicken broth
1/2 cup red wine
2 tablespoons dried parsley
A sprinkle of dried oregano or marjoram
Freshly grated Parmesan cheese
A few fresh basil leaves torn up by hand
A handful of cherry tomatoes

1. To roast the mushrooms, place them caps down on a non-stick baking pan. Sprinkle them with 2 tbsp olive oil, pepper and sea salt and bake at 375ºF for 20 minutes.

2. While the mushrooms are baking, roll the chicken thighs in a mix of flour with salt, pepper & oregano. Brown them in margarine or butter to seal in the juices.

3. As the chicken is browning, sprinkle with Herbes de Provence. Take the meat out when browned, and stir the chopped onion in the meat drippings with 2 tsp of olive oil. Fry them for 4-5 minutes, until they are soft and clear, then stir in the chopped garlic and cook for 1 minute. The garlic gets a shorter time as you don't want it browned.

4. Add the wine to the onions & garlic and stir making sure to stir up the browned bits on the bottom of the pan. Then add the can of chopped tomatoes followed by the chicken broth. Bring to a boil, reduce the temperature and cook for 10 minutes.

5. Return the chicken to the wine-tomato sauce adding the parsley and the oregano or marjoram and the mushrooms. A few of the basil leaves can be added at this time too. Bring the entire mix to a boil then reduce to a simmer and let cook for 20 – 25 minutes until the chicken is tender.

6. After transferring the cacciatore to a serving bowl, place cherry tomatoes loosely around it and sprinkle the basil leaf pieces on top.

We served it on Kjielkje (recipe below) sprinkled with fresh Parmesan, but it works well on rice or on a bed of fresh spinach leaves.

Chicken Cacciatore

Kjielkje

(Mennonite handmade noodles)

Ingredients:

Use a ratio of 1 egg to 1 cup of flour
milk sprinkled in as needed

1. Make a hill of flour on a smooth working surface. Create a small bowl-like opening in the top of the hill of flour (much like a volcano) to put the egg(s) in.

2. Using a fork, stir the egg from the top centre of the pile, pulling the flour into the egg slowly for it to blend. Continue stirring the flour into the egg and sprinkle milk as needed until it is all mixed together and feels like a thick dough.

3. Roll out the pasta dough until it is about 1/3 inch thick. Add flour to keep it from sticking to the surface.

4. Cut the pasta into strips and boil until tender. It will be a thick, rough type of pasta with a soft texture and it will taste dee-lish! A less healthy option is to fry the noodles up after boiling them. Yum!

From Our Family to Yours!

A few months ago, my daughter Daren and I spent a day with Mom where we made her chicken cacciatore and reminisced. We were joined by my Aunt Esther, her daughter Leanne and Leanne's daughter Beth. Esther brought some of Grandma's cook books and recipes and we enjoyed an afternoon of sharing memories and hearing some of the old family stories.

The six of us represented the only maternal lines descended from my grandmother, Elizabeth Voth Nickel Dyck. Betty and Esther were the two daughters of Elizabeth who had a daughter, who also had a daughter.

In the photo below, left to right, we are Esther, me, Betty, Daren, Leanne and Beth.

Cheers!
Carla

Chicken Cacciatore

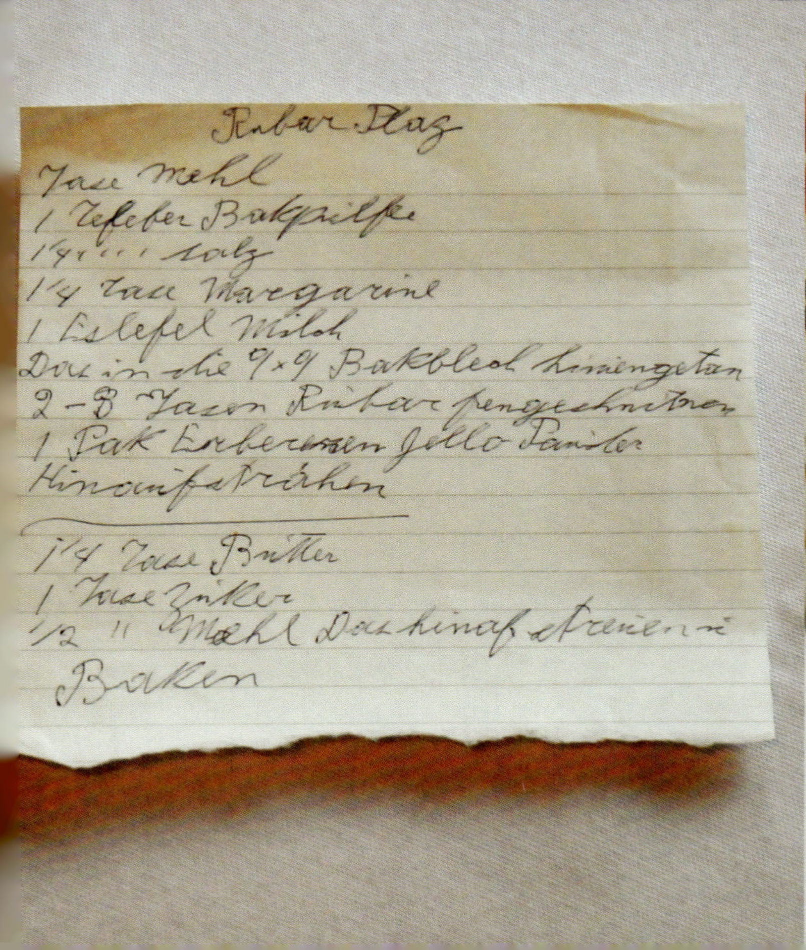

Rubar Plaz
Tase Mehl
1 Teleffel Bakpulfer
1/4 " " salz
1/4 tase Margarine
1 Eslefel Milch
Das in die 9×9 Bakblech hineingetan
2-3 Tasen Rubar fenngeschnitten
1 Pak Erdbeeren Jello Pulver
Hinaufstreuen

1/4 Tase Butter
1 Tase Zucker
1/2 " Mehl Das hinauf streuen
Baken

Why did Grandma call it "Sin" ?

My grandmother was a devout Mennonite woman. Specifically, she was Mennonite Brethren. As long as she was able, she woke up at 5 am to bake buns everyday. Her kitchen was uniquely equipped with a special large flour bin for all her baking. She was very clear about what was right and wrong in her mind. She out-lived two husbands and always called things the way she saw them. Alcohol was not touched under any conditions. It was "sin."

Humans have enjoyed "sin" of many different kinds for many different reasons. We linger over the subtle nuances of a fine wine and we readily embrace the thirst-quenching qualities of a great beer on a hot day. Non-alcoholic versions of wine and beer serve a purpose, but are not adequate substitutes. The "sin" is essential to the taste and the overall enjoyment of a drink.

Alcohol and fermenting have been an essential part of the human diet in cultures around the globe throughout human history. "Sin" has been a source of nutrition, a source of inspiration and it has also been a source of destruction. We associate alcohol with both great joys and with deep sorrows.

Our attitude toward alcohol swings to the extreme ends of the spectrum. Some communities and religions insist on total abstinence, while others incorporate it into daily life and religious celebrations.

None of this is new. Alcohol, its production and consumption, is woven throughout human history. Pottery jars were found in an ancient Chinese grave that had contained brew residues from around 7000 BC. It had been a fermented drink made from rice, honey, grapes and hawthorn berries. Pottery fragments from 6000 BC in southern Russia, that used to contain wine, were decorated with images of people raising their arms in celebration. Slaves who built some of the Egyptian pyramids were given large daily rations of beer. It was treated mostly as a food, but the beer recipe of the time had about 5% alcohol by volume making each slave essentially a functioning alcoholic by today's standards.

The people of ancient Greece had an interesting attitude toward "sin." They considered it improper to give a public speech without drinking a little before hand. They believed sober speakers were too logical and lacked passion.

The early leaders of the Roman empire, on the other hand, were nervous about alcohol. Women and young men were not allowed to drink and the followers of Bacchus, who believed drunkenness was essential to worship, were persecuted and nearly 7,000 of them lost their lives. Over time, though, vineyards were planted all over the empire and wine eventually became a part of daily life.

A recently as the early 1920's, Prohibition in the U.S. tried to eliminate alcohol in the country altogether, but it created more problems than it solved, so it was repealed. There remain some communities though that are "dry" and successfully so.

Alcohol has served humanity as food, as medicine, as entertainment, as a pleasure, as a danger and even as a form of worship. Depending on the time, place, culture and religion you are a part of, you will view alcohol as one or a combination of any of the above.

My devout grandmother believed to the depths of her soul that alcohol was dangerous and she simply called it "sin." While I find the phrase charming today, she did not and she was very serious about it. It wasn't until her very senior years that she let herself have a little night cap to help her sleep. In the same way that human attitudes changed over time, so did my dear grandmother's.

My German grandmother probably never knew this one, but this old German rhyme says it well.

Der grösste Feind des Menschens voll, das ist und bleibt der Alkohol.
Doch, in der Bibel steht geschrieben, Du sollst auch deine Feinde lieben.

The translation is:

The greatest enemy of the wellbeing of mankind is and remains alcohol.
However in the Bible it is written you shall also love your enemies.

Whether it is a mixed cocktail, a micro-brew, a shot of hard liquor, home-made hooch or a spiked coffee for dessert, many are willing to pay the "sin" tax that comes with it. Cooking may burn off a lot of the alcohol, and may make it less *sin*ful, yet there is a twinkle in the eye of each person who finds a new way to incorporate alcohol into a dish.

Carla, her husband Steve & her Grandma - late 1980's

"Cool Poor" Champagne Squash Soup

Squash Soup

Champagne makes you feel like it's Sunday and better days are just around the corner.
~ Marlene Deitrich

Barry Lane and Tara Park Lane found themselves far away from family and friends when they moved to the quiet snowy cottage town early in the new year. They had both quit their jobs and moved to this small town for school. To brighten up their compact, generic apartment, they filled it with a mish-mash of hand-me-downs, wedding gifts and furniture for which they had scrimped and saved. There was a rag rug from Ikea, a wobbly wooden dinner table that had belonged to Barry's great-grandmother, and two wooden adirondack chairs. One chair was painted yellow and the other was a loud blue. They weren't allowed to paint the boring white walls, so they covered them with pictures. The place was jammed full.

Tara and Barry knew they were poor. While they found it challenging to adjust to their new economic situation, they decided that the poor situation they were in had some "cool" aspects to it, so they decided to call themselves "cool poor."

Tara and Barry's "cool poor" was not the living-paycheque-to-paycheque, no-holiday-in-Mexico-this-year kind of poor. Theirs was the no-paycheque-at-all kind of poor. They couldn't even "splurge" on a $3.49 plastic milk container. Instead, they poured the milk bags into a beautiful yellow and green pottery pitcher that had been a wedding gift from Uncle John and Aunt Shelly.

As beautiful as the pitcher was, it didn't pour very well and the milk could be unpleasant to drink because it always absorbed the odours of the previous night's leftovers. The milk had a different flavour every time they tasted it. It was hard to enjoy.

One day in the spring, Tara saw Barry bicycling home toward her with one arm in the air, waving something blue in his hand. As he got closer, Tara realized the blue thing in his hand was a blue plastic milk container. Yes, blue, not boring white. It had a piece of ripped off scotch tape on it with "25 cents" written in black marker. Barry had talked the guy at the yard sale down to ten cents for it!

A few weeks after they moved in, Tara's parents called to say they were going to swing by their place for a visit on their way home from a holiday. Tara looked for something yummy, warm and cozy to make them for lunch to stave off the winter's chill. She found a recipe called "Champagne Squash Soup."

Tara and her mom both loved squash, so she knew it was the meal to make. The cheapest bottle of champagne would be half their grocery money for the week, but it was something they knew they had to do. They splurged, bought the champagne and made the soup.

Tara remembers standing in her small kitchen at the tiny apartment-sized stove, with the oven that never really worked, sautéing the onions in butter and adding the champagne. The aroma is sweetly embedded in her memory.

The four of them sat on uncomfortable fold-out chairs at the wobbly wooden table and enjoyed the soup and their precious time together. Since they could barely afford the soup, there wasn't much else with the meal except a fresh loaf of bread from the bread maker, (another wedding gift), and the remainder of the champagne. They cherished every sip.

Tara and Barry have made this soup many times since. They now have children and own their own home in a larger city. They can afford a nicer bottle of champagne. While they are also able to serve more with it, they say it is best served with a thick slice of warm olive bread generously spread with butter that has melted into it. Don't forget a nice glass of bubbly, too!

And that milk jug? ... it still sits in their fridge hugging a bag of milk to this day.

Squash Sou

"Cool Poor" Champagne Squash Soup

Serves 6-8

Ingredients:

4 lbs. squash, acorn or butternut
2 medium onions, halved & thinly sliced
4 tablespoons butter (2 + 2)
1/4 cup champagne
4-5 cups chicken broth
1/2 teaspoon. nutmeg
salt & pepper to taste
1/4 cup sour cream

Preheat oven to 350ºF. Line a cookie sheet with foil.

1. Quarter the squash and scoop out the seeds. Place the quarters skin-side up on the cookie sheet and bake 1 - 1 1/2 hours until the squash is tender.

2. Let the squash cool. Scoop out the pulp and purée in batches in a food processor.

3. Sauté the onions in 2 tablespoons of the butter until they turn clear. Add the champagne and cook, stirring often, until liquid is absorbed and onions are golden brown. Purée the onions in a food processor with a little of the squash purée.

4. In a large saucepan, combine the onion and squash purées. Whisk in the chicken broth until you reach the consistency you prefer.

5. Cover and heat on medium, stirring occasionally. Whisk in the final 2 tablespoons of butter. Season with nutmeg, salt and pepper.

6. To decorate, fill individual bowls with the soup, drop a small spoonful of sour cream on top of each bowl and swirl with a knife. Sprinkle a pinch of nutmeg on top and you can garnish with a sprig of fresh parsley.

"Ci Vediamo"

Spezzatino

spezzatino

Wine makes every meal an occasion, every table more elegant, every day more civilized.
~ Andre Simon

Heather Kleim had just moved to Florence, Italy and even though she knew a bit of Italian, she found out the hard way how literal translations can go awry.

"See you later!" is a very common English phrase and is often used very casually. It is not meant literally. Well, Heather learned that the hard way during her first days in Florence. After saying good bye to a friend, she threw in a "Ci vediamo dopo!" and headed home for the day.

Later that night, Heather received a phone call from my friend who was a little irritated. "You said you'd see me later! Where are you?" Oops. Lesson learned. "Ci vediamo" (minus the 'dopo' meaning 'later') would have worked and prevented insulting anyone.

Heather's roommate Laura was a wonderful cook from Dublin. The two of them worked long days and sometimes on a cold winter night, Laura would cook them a pot of Spezzatino and they would hunker down to a comfortable evening of watching English DVDs. A comfortable friend in a comfortable place with comfortable food and a comfortable language.

Spezzatino is a Tuscan stew of minced or diced meat. It can be found in almost every restaurant and deli throughout Florence, but is not as common outside of Tuscany. Heather says, "Spezzatino is stew at its finest. Throw this into a pot and let the simmering do its magic!"

Spezzatino

“Ci Vediamo” Spezzatino

Serves 4

Ingredients:

2 carrots, finely chopped
2 celery stalks, finely chopped
1 onion, finely chopped
2 large potatoes, peeled, cut into large pieces
2 lbs stewing beef, cut into 1-inch cubes (900g)
1/2 cup of olive oil (120ml)
3 cups of red wine (710ml)
1/2 cup tomato purée (120ml)
salt and fresh black pepper to season

1. In a large stewing pot, heat extra virgin olive oil and sear beef for a few minutes. Season with salt and pepper.

2. Remove beef from the pot and add carrots, celery, and onions. Cook for 2 minutes or until vegetables have become soft.

3. Add 1 cup of red wine and let reduce.

4. Add the potatoes to the pot and season with salt and pepper.

5. Return the seared beef to the pot then add tomato purée and the remaining wine.

6. Let the liquid come to a boil and reduce the heat to medium. Simmer for an hour and a half and serve.

"Roman Holiday"
Spaghetti Carbonara

carbonara

Reporter: Which of the cities visited did Your Highness enjoy the most?
Princess Ann: Each, in its own way, was unforgettable. It would be difficult to... Rome! By all means, Rome. I will cherish my visit here in memory as long as I live.
~ Excerpt from the movie Roman Holiday (1953)

Many years ago (I won't give a number!), I used to babysit three truly adorable young kids, Simon, Sarah and Mark. Simon was always pensive and intellectual. He liked to discuss things, while Mark the baby did what most babies did - ate, slept and pooped! Sarah was quite charming and had a special sparkle in her eye. She figured things out really quickly and would often return your knowing glance with a coy smile.

After I left home for university, three more beautiful children joined the family, Rachel, Ruth and David. Of course they have all grown up now. Simon, Sarah and Mark are all married and have moved even further away. Mark, the baby, has really grown UP. Long ago he topped my 6' 2" height and he now hovers somewhere around a mere 6' 9".

When Sarah contacted me and told me she had a recipe, I was so pleased. It was wonderful to reconnect and catch up. She now has two children of her own, James and Elizabeth, and even though her husband's name is actually Jeremy, she sometimes just calls him "Handsome."

When their first child James was just four months old, Sarah and Jeremy Fresz decided it was time to visit her extended family in England. Adding an extra excursion to Rome and Paris was natural for the two history buffs. As Sarah explained it, "Rome because of the history and Paris, well... who doesn't want to go to Paris? And the price was right!"

Walking through the Coliseum and the Roman Forum were Sarah and Jeremy's favourite moments. So much had happened there that continues to impact the world today. "It was awe-inspiring and overwhelming to stand there and think about all that had happened... to imagine Caesar, and Nero, and the other emperors in their fine robes walking amongst the pillars." She also pondered the prisoners and imagined some of the well-known Christian prisoners like the apostles Peter and Paul walking through the streets in chains.

Then there was the food. Sarah and Jeremy share the Italian love of delicious food: the pastas, the meats and the breads dipped in olive oil with balsamic vinegar. They had so much fun trying out different restaurants and all different kinds of food. They especially fell in love with Spaghetti Carbonara the way the Italians make it.

As Sarah explains it, "True carbonara has eggs in it! The American version is more saucy... almost an Alfredo sauce. That is so wrong!"

When they returned home, Sarah and Jeremy were bound and determined to recreate the spaghetti in the authentic way. They found a recipe that was close and had a lot of fun adjusting the ingredients to get it right. They added garlic and that brought it closer. But the key ingredient that it needed was white wine. "It made all the difference in the world!"

Carbonara

"Roman Holiday" Spaghetti Carbonara

Serves 8

Ingredients:

1 pound spaghetti
1 tablespoon olive oil
8 slices bacon, diced
1 tablespoon olive oil
1 onion, chopped
1 clove garlic, minced
1/4 cup dry white wine
4 eggs
1/2 cup grated Parmesan cheese
1 pinch salt and black pepper to taste
2 tablespoons chopped fresh parsley
2 tablespoons grated Parmesan cheese

1. In a large pot of boiling salted water, cook spaghetti pasta until al dente. Drain well. Toss with 1 tablespoon of olive oil, and set aside.

2. Meanwhile in a large skillet, cook chopped bacon until slightly crisp; remove and drain onto paper towels. Reserve 2 tablespoons of bacon fat in the pan, add remaining 1 tablespoon olive oil and heat in reused large skillet. Add chopped onion, and cook over medium heat until onion is translucent. Add minced garlic, and cook 1 minute more, being careful not to over-cook it. Add wine; cook one more minute.

3. Return cooked bacon to pan; add cooked and drained spaghetti. Toss to coat and heat through, adding more olive oil if it seems dry or is sticking together.

4. Add beaten eggs and cook, tossing constantly with tongs or large fork until eggs are BARELY set. It may be wise to take it off the heat first so the eggs don't fry. Quickly add 1/2 cup Parmesan cheese, and toss again. Add salt and pepper to taste.

5. Serve immediately with chopped parsley sprinkled on top, and extra Parmesan cheese at table.

Sarah's Tip:

"If the eggs "scramble" when you're cooking them, you've overcooked them. Its a bit difficult to get them just right. Err on just under-cooking it as they will keep cooking in the dish as you serve it."

carbonara

"Golden Apple" Roasted Rabbit

Roasted Rabbit

Days of wine and roses laugh and run away,
Like a child at play.
~ Johnny Mercer

By Chef Suman

With a lovely view of the Bay of Fundy, Grand Pré Estates Winery makes Nova Scotia wine in the beautiful Annapolis Valley. Their stately rows of grapevines grow unique grapes that have been designed to thrive in the particular growing climate of Annapolis Valley. Instead of growing Old World varieties like Chardonnay or Sauvignon, Grand Pré strongly believes that new wine producing regions should develop and perfect their own varieties, styles and vineyard practices to make wines that are born of and unique to their region. Not only does this create a truly Nova Scotia wine, but it makes it easier to grow the grapes without the costly and sometimes environmentally damaging methods needed to grow non-indigenous strains.

Grand Pré is the oldest winery in Nova Scotia. It was started in the 1970s by Roger Dial, who is considered the pioneer of Nova Scotia winemaking. He ran the winery until 1993 when it was purchased by Hanspeter Stutz. Stutz wanted to create not just wine but also a tourism experience, by renovating the grounds and offering vineyard tours in the summer and fall. They still make wines with their special grapes, but they now also offer unique varieties like ice wine and their very special Pomme d'Or.

Pomme d'Or means "golden apple" in French and is a particularly apt name for this wine. The rich golden hue combines with the sweetness almost of an ice wine to make it seem like you really are drinking sweet liquid gold. Made from six varieties of apples grown in the Annapolis Valley (Macintosh, Cortland, Russet, Northern Spy, and two secret varieties), the mix of old and new strains give the flavour and bouquet a complexity that makes it stand apart. The notes of baked apple, apricot and caramel pair beautifully with the saddle of rabbit and bring an unmistakable flavour to the marinade. Just make sure to save a few glasses for yourself.

Recipe Courtesy : "From Pemmican To Poutine – A Journey through Canada's Culinary History" by Chef Suman

Roasted Rabbi

Grand Pré

“Golden Apple” Roasted Rabbit Marinated in Grand Pre’s Pomme D’Or

Serves 6

Marinade:
1 cup Grand Pre’s Pomme D’Or
2 cups chicken stock
1/4 teaspoon ground nutmeg
1/4 teaspoon fresh tarragon, finely chopped
1 teaspoon garlic, finely chopped
1 teaspoon shallot, finely chopped
1 tablespoon chili pepper flakes
1 teaspoon salt
1 teaspoon black pepper, freshly ground

Meat:
2 rabbits, 2 lbs. each

Roasting Vegetables:
3 sweet potatoes, 5 cm (2”) diced
2 carrots, peeled and 5 cm (2”) diced
1 celery stalk, 5 cm (2”) diced
1 onion, 5 cm (2”) diced
1 bay leaf

1. In a large mixing bowl, mix together all of the ingredients for the marinade and marinate both rabbits overnight in a refrigerator.

2. Preheat the oven to 300ºF.

3. In a roasting pan layer the bottom with the large diced vegetables, and place the 2 rabbits on top. Reserve any leftover marinade.

4. Roast in the oven covered for 3 hours until cooked through, basting occasionally with the leftover marinade. You will know it is cooked when the meat is almost falling off the bones.

5. Increase the oven temperature to 400ºF and remove the cover to get an even golden brown colour on the rabbits.

6. Serve the rabbits with the vegetables and the juices from the pan.

Find out more about Chef Suman & Grand Pré Winery at www.CookingWithSin.com.

"Comfort of Home" Sherry Potatoes

Sherry Potatoes

If penicillin can cure those that are ill,
Spanish sherry can bring the dead back to life.
~ Sir Alexander Fleming

George is a well respected and charismatic engineering technologist. He has been happily married to Tabitha for seventeen years and they have two gorgeous daughters. They prefer to call their girls by their pet names. Their five-year old is "Moo-moo" and the two-year old is "Beezer."

George is known for his energy and hilarious sense of fun. He laughs often and loudly and is the first suspect in an office prank. He and Tabitha are often the last to leave a party and George is notorious for ripping up the dance floor.

The home George has made for himself and his family is very different from the one he was raised in. Before he turned two, his parents divorced and his mom spiralled into schizophrenia, so George had to live with his grandparents. While his grandparents cared for him deeply, they found George's energy challenging. By the time he was in middle school he had become quite a handful. He also discovered that he had a terrific sense of humour and used it effectively if he got in trouble.

On a particularly challenging day in Grade 9, one of his teachers got frustrated with him and sent him out of the room. The teacher expected George to wait in the hall. Instead he made his way to the courtyard just outside the room. When the teacher realized George was mocking him through the windows, he called in the principal. The courtyard only had two access doors, so the principal came out one door and the teacher was at the other. They were certain they had George cornered.

Relying on his rule "If you get in trouble, it's more interesting if you're funny," George started running around. It must have seemed like a scene out of a funny movie. George was running around the courtyard and giggling while the principal and teacher chased him. All the while, the kids in every class that overlooked the courtyard had their noses pressed against the glass, laughing and cheering for their destined-for-detention hero. George never finished high school; he didn't even finish Grade 9.

George spent the next 10 years swinging from job to job, to evening school and back to another job again and again. He was directionless and often in trouble. Finally, his grandparents ran out of options and kicked him out. After a failed attempt to once again live with his mother, George moved into Tabitha's family's home. Tabitha's family had their own struggles, however. At the ripe age of seventeen George and Tabitha knew they were better on their own, so they moved out.

When George was twenty and Tabitha was eighteen, they got married. The odds were stacked precariously against the young couple. George's job prospects were limited and they had no one but themselves to rely on. The two of them did have one thing in their favour; they were dreamers. They believed they could create something better than what they had been shown.

By the time George turned twenty-five, he and Tabitha had established a solid home for themselves. He knew he was ready for further training and he got admitted to a reputable engineering technologist program under the school's mature student program.

Today, George and Tabitha have created a solid, loving home. What they needed but were not given in their youth, they have created for themselves and their daughters. They defied all the odds and have become enormously successful in all areas of their lives and they are still dreaming. Last year they bought their first investment property and have now become landlords. The sky truly is the limit for them, yet the joys and comforts of home are what mean the most.

George and Tabitha cherish family meals together and he loves these sherry potatoes so much, he enthusiastically shares the recipe with his workmates. These potatoes are a true comfort food. He says to be sure to cover all the potatoes well with the sherry and butter mix.

"Comfort of Home" Sherry Potoatoes

Serves 3-4

Ingredients:

Olive oil spray
3-4 medium sized potatoes cut thin into 1/4" slices (1/2 cm)
1/2 cup melted butter
1/2 cup dry sherry
salt and pepper

1. Layer the sliced potatoes in a casserole dish that was sprayed with olive oil.

2. Mix the melted butter and sherry together and pour the mixture over the potatoes. Be sure to cover the potatoes well. Add salt and pepper to taste.

3. Bake uncovered at 375ºF for an hour.

"Stuck on Reduction" Grilled Watermelon Salad

with Madeira Caramel

watermelon

Five years before the Boston Tea Party, there was the "Madeira Wine Party." A ship was smuggling Madeira wine for John Hancock, one of the politicians who would eventually sign the Declaration of Independence, and was seized by the British. A fight broke out. Hancock won and received his smuggled Madeira. This set the precedent for the Boston Tea Party.

He at first refus'd us peremptorily; but at dinner with his council, where there was great drinking of Madeira wine, as the custom of that place then was, he softened by degrees, and said he would lend us six. After a few more bumpers he advanc'd to ten; and at length he very good-naturedly conceded eighteen.

~ Ben Franklin, 1744, asking Governor Clinton of NY for more cannon power in Boston.

What gravy is to English cuisine, demi-glace is to French cuisine. French cuisine has a few select "mother sauces" that are the bases of all other sauces - bechamel, velouté, espagnole, tomato and hollandaise.

Espagnole is the Mother Sauce for demi-glace. Demi-glace is basically beef stock reduced. The industry standard is fifty percent beef stock, fifty percent sauce espagnol reduced by half.

When Chef Tim Wasylko was in culinary school, the demi-glace classes piqued his interest. He was enthralled by what happens when liquids are reduced down. The liquids are evaporated and the flavours become concentrated. He began experimenting by reducing all the liquids he encountered. He made adult snow cones from a reduction of blueberry juice and Cabernet wine. Then he made a port-wine caramel to put on ice cream.

Chef Tim says, "Madeira port-- a fortified sweet booze that reduces down to a wonderful caramel -- awesome on ice cream -- or banana tempura split... Go get a bottle of Madeira -- and reduce it down to a caramel -- its life changing."

"Stuck on Reduction" Watermelon Salad with Asparagus and Madeira Caramel

Serves 4

Ingredients:

1/2 medium-sized seedless watermelon
1 teaspoon kosher salt
1/2 teaspoon cracked black pepper
1/4 cup good quality olive oil
1 lime, juiced
1 bunch fresh mint leaves, chopped
1 bunch fresh basil leaves, chopped
24 stalks of asparagus
200g goat cheese.
1 bottle of Madeira

1. Pour bottle of Madeira in a large pot and place over moderate heat. Bring to a boil and allow to boil hard for approximately 20 minutes or until it has reduced down to slightly less than a 1/4 cup. It should coat the back of a spoon and be nice and thick. It will thicken more as it cools. Let it cool. Once cool, pour into a plastic squeeze bottle.

2. Cut watermelon into 4 square shapes approximately 5 cm by 3 cm thick. Season with salt and pepper, lime juice, oil, mint and basil. Toss and let rest one hour. Reserve the marinade.

3. Place the watermelon pieces on a high BBQ grill for 1 minute per side. Allow to cool.

4. Blanch the asparagus and cut in 7 cm long pieces. They should all be the same size.

5. Shape goat cheese in rounds or rolls 2-3 cm in diameter. Cut into medallions.

6. To assemble, toss the asparagus in the marinade from the watermelon. Put 6 pieces of asparagus tight together - and perfectly lined up - down the centre of a plate. Then place the grilled watermelon on top of the asparagus in the opposite direction. Place 2 slices of goat cheese on top and make a zig zag design of the Madeira caramel in the squeeze bottle over top.

Find out more about Chef Tim Wasylko at www.CookingWithSin.com.

"Takin' the Piss" Crisper Sangria

sangria

Balmy days, sweet sangria.
She's been gone, have you seen her?
Señorita shyly turning away,
Leaving me our fading flame.
~ Tori Amos "Sweet Sangria"

By Michelle Johnson

I answer the phone and an English accent calls out, "Get your dimply ass over here. The sangria is ready!" My heart fills with love. I put on my lipstick and dash out the door knowing that soon Martin's cozy kitchen will be noisy with laughter and frivolity. Upon my arrival, someone announces, "The wife's here!" It's a label I earned due to my tendency to lean on him. The guest list could have filled a mansion so this party spills out onto the lawn.

Martin is like an oak tree that allows all kinds of strange birds to perch on his branches. Lucky enough to be one of those birds, I'm greeted with a huge warm hug. Martin says, "Go on, Love. Serve yourself a tall glass. You gotta catch up - it's in the crisper!"

The nibbly food is out for munching, the BBQ is ready and the fridge is filled to capacity. I nudge my way over to the fridge, grab a glass and slide open the crisper drawer. Oh! A beautiful array of colour awaits. Scooping it out with the soup ladle the glass quickly cools my hand. One sip and I know it's gonna be a fun and "oh so messy" evening.

Martin Poyser, a dear friend, a keeper of secrets, a partner in crime and expert when it comes to "Takin' the piss." This recipe for Crisper Sangria is one of the lessons I learned from him.

Carla's note:

Michelle is my sister. I'll never forget the darkness in her voice when she told me her best friend, Martin Poyser, had suddenly died of a heart condition. The shock in her voice echoed the pain of having part of her heart torn away. Martin had filled a special place in her life and he could never be replaced.

Michelle and Martin were a marvellous two-some, supporting each other's ups and downs, and always laughing boisterously through it all. Michelle always said that Gordon Ramsey, the "Hell's Kitchen" chef, was remarkably similar to Martin. Their energy, passion, fiery tongues and British accents along with their physical similarities were uncanny.

The love they had for each other was more profound than a romantic love. Martin helped Michelle navigate her new world of singleness after her separation, treating her to meals and pampering her any way he could. Michelle appreciated the stability of Martin's relationship with his partner, Martin. Yes, two Martins! You can see the sparkle and joy in all their eyes in the beautiful photo. They knew how to have fun!

If you're not British, you might be curious to learn that "Takin' The Piss" is an old phrase that means to mock or express disbelief.

Crisper

"Takin' The Piss" Sangria

Martin taught me many things, mostly by example.
Here is one of the lessons I learned.

1. Invite everybody over to your house - trust me, it'll be fine.
2. Throw out your vegetables.
3. Clean your fridge crisper drawer so it gleams a welcoming shine.
4. Line the bottom with fruit - raspberries, strawberries, oranges, pineapple, lemons, kiwis, blueberries, plum, grapes.
5. Add some spirit - cover the fruit with brandy or whisky, add a splash of triple sec.
6. Let that sit for an hour or two... resist the urge to nibble or the guests will be hungry and you will be too tipsy to care.
7. Add your favourite cheap and cheerful red wine to fill the crisper 2/3's from the top.
8. Add some sparkly water or lemony pop to add some fizz.
9. If you are a bitter person, add sugar.
10. Using a soup ladle, serve, toast, sip and ... at every chance you get, lovingly "take the piss."

Keep up with all the sharing.
Sign up for the "Cooking With Sin" Newsletter at www.CookingWithSin.com.

Crisper

Wine Aroma Wheel

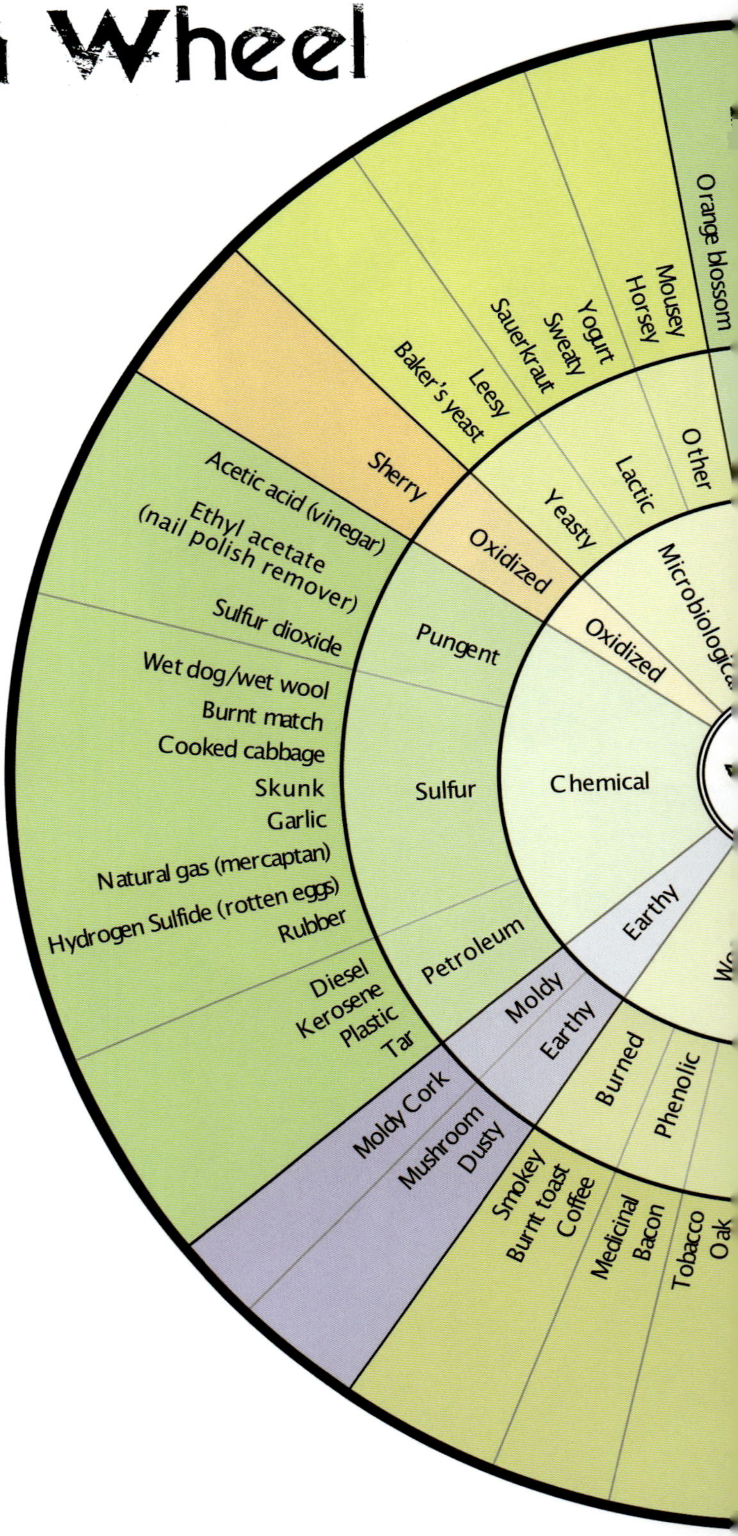

Aroma Wheel

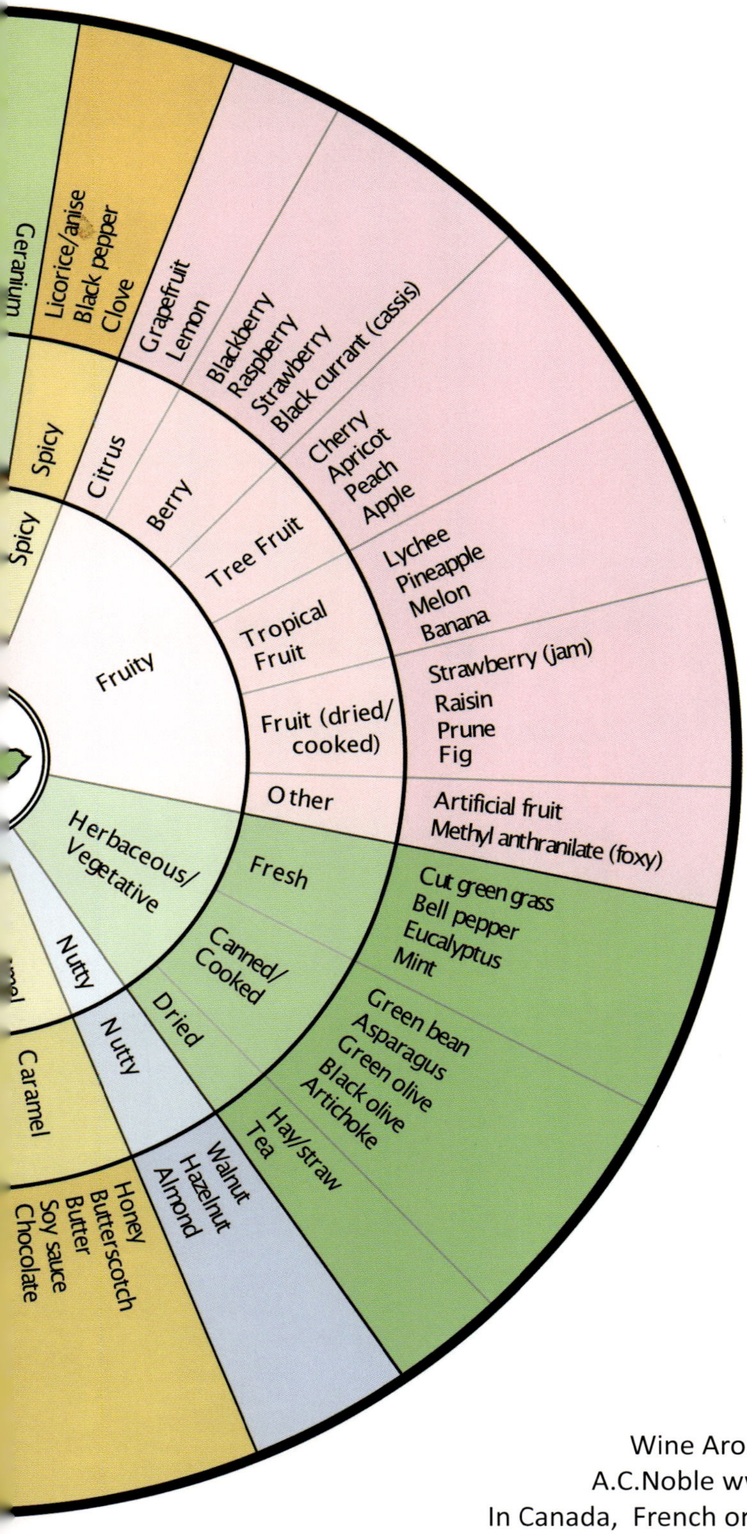
Fruity
Citrus
Grapefruit
Lemon
Berry
Blackberry
Raspberry
Strawberry
Black currant (cassis)
Tree Fruit
Cherry
Apricot
Peach
Apple
Tropical Fruit
Lychee
Pineapple
Melon
Banana
Fruit (dried/ cooked)
Strawberry (jam)
Raisin
Prune
Fig
Other
Artificial fruit
Methyl anthranilate (foxy)
Herbaceous/ Vegetative
Fresh
Cut green grass
Bell pepper
Eucalyptus
Mint
Canned/ Cooked
Green bean
Asparagus
Green olive
Black olive
Artichoke
Dried
Hay/straw
Tea
Nutty
Nutty
Walnut
Hazelnut
Almond
Caramel
Honey
Butterscotch
Butter
Soy sauce
Chocolate
Spicy
Spicy
Licorice/anise
Black pepper
Clove
Geranium

EXOTIC
SOUR PUSS
BOMBAY SAPPHIRE
NOTIQ

spirits
&
liqueurs

"Special Delivery" Black Forest Cake

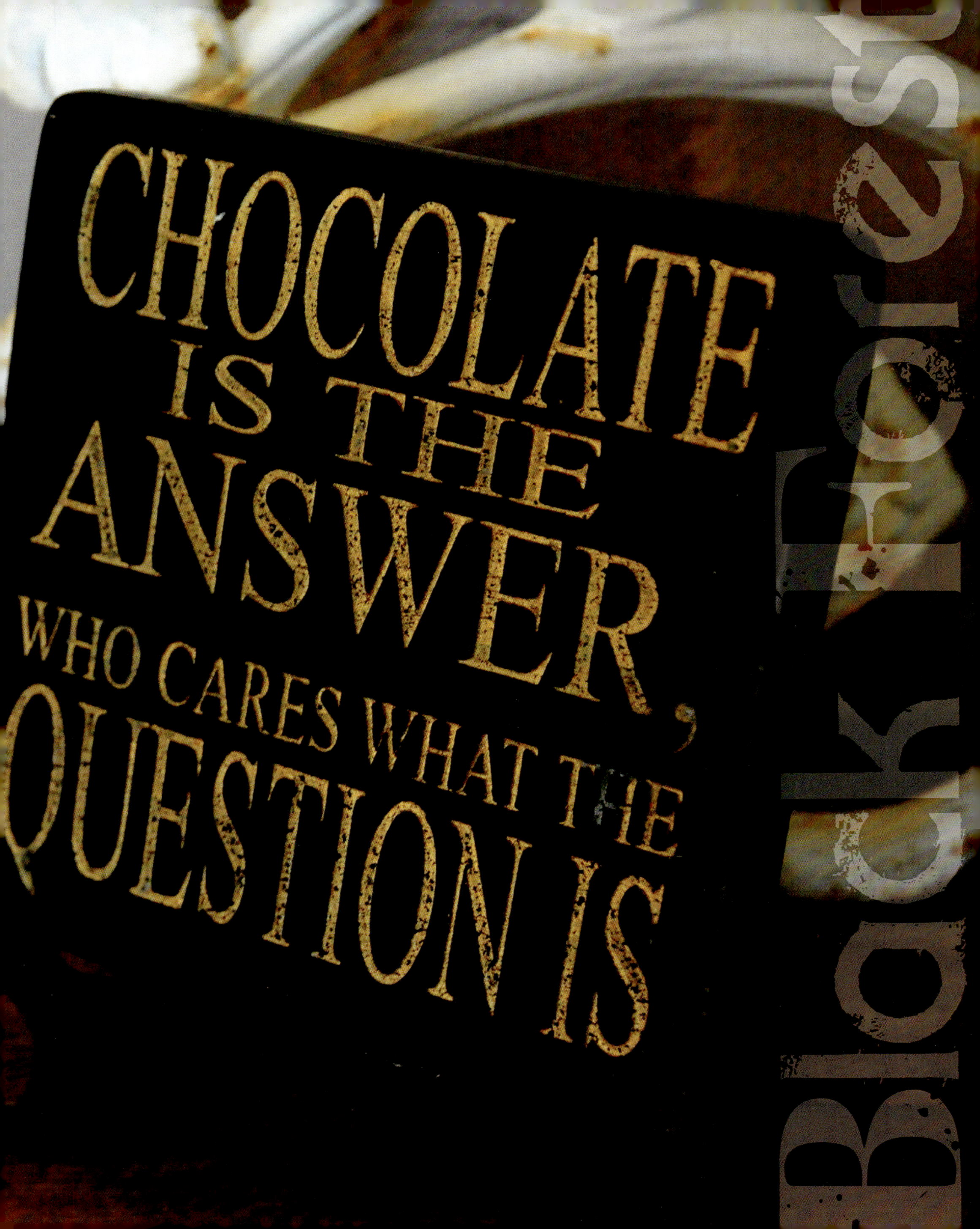
CHOCOLATE
IS THE
ANSWER,
WHO CARES WHAT THE
QUESTION IS

Claret is the liquor for boys; port for men;
but he who aspires to be a hero must drink brandy.
~ Samuel Johnson

Shelley (Boyd) Stone is my dear friend and neighbour. She has done many things with her boundless energy and creativity over the years. After studying theology, she worked with young people on the streets, in high schools and as a camp director at Pioneer Camp. When her children were young, she ran a great daycare out of her home where she cared for our daughter. When her kids got older she worked in a local college. Then, a few years ago, she found her dream job - I called it her "Erin Brokovich job" - coordinating the efforts of the Ontario chapter of the non-profit organization "Gleaners."

Gleaners takes in surplus vegetables and fruit from farms. Volunteers prepare the fruit and vegetables before it is dried and made into a soup mix. The soup mixes are sent all over the world to areas of need, such as refugees camps and crisis areas. After the earthquake in Haiti, she worked over-time to direct extra food to the relief efforts there.

Our paths have crossed repeatedly for the past twenty-five plus years. One New Year's Eve, I spent the afternoon with Shelley and her two children, Victoria and Tyler. She had just finished making her mother's Black Forest cake with brandy. We took a moment to sit and catch up over a piece of cake. It was delicious!

Shelley's parents Bill and Jean Boyd were actively involved in their church and, true to their beliefs, faithful abstainers. There was one exception. Jean loved to make her Black Forest cake with brandy. Jean loved to cook and especially enjoyed desserts, but her Black Forest cake was a favourite for special occasions. In Ontario, liquor is only sold in government controlled stores called the LCBO (Liquor Control Board of Ontario). Shopping for brandy would have been strongly looked down upon by her fellow church members, so Jean would don, what she called, her "Jackie O" outfit. She hoped that the scarf over her head and the large sunglasses would make her unrecognizable on her trip to the LCBO.

In the fall of 1981, Shelley was in her second year at Bible College. Shelley remembers her time at college with true fondness. She made a lot of great friends and had a wonderful time, but the college had rules and expectations in the eighties that would shock most students there today. Female students had to wear dresses or skirts to all classes. Dorm supervisors had to be notified any time students left the campus. Everyone had to sign in for breakfast and all dorms had to have lights out by 11 pm. Dancing and drinking were absolutely prohibited.

Undaunted, Jean decided that Shelley's birthday that fall would not be complete without her special Black Forest cake with brandy. Jean baked the cake, soaked it in brandy and arranged it carefully along with all the accessories in a special package. She then took special precautions and had it sent to Shelley by bus. Jean chose the bus because she was concerned it would get too jostled in the mail. When Shelley heard her cake was en route, she didn't ask permission of her dorm supervisor. Instead she simply told her, "My mom is sending me a brandy cake for my birthday and I am eating it." Jean has since passed away - gone too soon. She was always fun, energetic, wise and full of adventure. I am so pleased to share her Black Forest cake recipe with you. It's a great way to honour a truly wonderful woman.

Relax

"Special Delivery" Black Forest Cake

Serves 8-10

Ingredients:

1 chocolate cake mix
1 can cherry pie filling
1 can (398 mL) drained bing cherries
3 oz. Brandy
500 ml whipped ceam
1/4 cup sugar
1 teaspoon vanilla extract
fresh cherries and chocolate shavings for garnish

1. Make the chocolate cake according to package directions, baking it in 2 round pans. When completely cooled, carefully cut both cakes in half horizontally, creating 4 rounds. A bread knife works well for this task.

   Tip: To make a straight cut, place toothpicks around the cake and use them to guide your cut.

2. In a bowl, combine the cherry pie filling with the drained bing cherries.

3. Whip the cream, adding sugar and vanilla extract.

4. With a fork, poke holes in each cake round, here and there on top of each layer. Drizzle an ounce of brandy over every layer and let it soak in.

6. Layer a sliced cake round, topped with 1/3 of the cherry mixture and a thin layer of whipped cream. Repeat twice.

7. Reserve plenty of whipped cream, cover the outside of the entire cake in it, then decorate the cake with the fresh cherries and chocolate shavings..

8. This cake stores best in the fridge to keep the whipped cream cold.

Find out how Shelley and the Gleaners helped out in the Haiti earthquake at www.CookingWithSin.com.

Black Fores

"Savoury Scent" Chicken Soup

chicken Soup

Behave so the aroma of your actions may enhance the general sweetness of the atmosphere.
~ Henry David Thoreau

Ada hari, ada nasi.
(Where there is a day, there is rice.)
~ Malaysian Proverb

H.T. Lam's mom learned to cook late in life. She grew up in Malaysia in a family where most of the household chores, such as cooking and cleaning, were done by live-in maids. It's the kind of thing most of us would envy. But, she gave all that up when she married for love. H.T. remembers how his family just scraped by when he was little. It was a good thing the cost of living was low.

H.T.'s dad worked as a linesman for a local hydro company in Malaysia. His mom liked to cook soups. They were easy to make and went well with rice, an inexpensive Malaysian staple.

One evening, many years ago when H.T. was young, his mom made this chicken soup for dinner. When he and his brother arrived home from school they smelled something "gamey." The boys asked their mom what the aroma was and she replied, "Chicken soup. Is there something wrong?"

"No," H.T. replied, "It just smells a bit strange."

H.T.'s mom had been home all day and had grown accustomed to the smell. She went into the garden for some fresh air and when she returned she noticed the smell! "Okay boys," she said, "we need to fix this before dad comes home! What can we do?"

She called her mom for help who told her to use three fingers of brandy. That did it! Dinner was saved!

This is the recipe that H.T.'s mom made that day. He likes to cook it to this day. It's quite simple and quite good.

Chicken Soup

"Savoury Scent" Chicken Soup

Serves 6

Ingredients:

1 whole chicken, with bones, remove fat and skin
4 large carrots, chopped to 1 inch chunks
4 yellow potatoes, chopped to 1 inch chunks
4 celery stalks, chopped to 1 inch chunks
2 cooking onions, quarters
sea salt
3 fingers of brandy

1. Combine all the ingredients into a stock pot and add water up to 3 inches (6 cm) above the ingredients.

2. Bring it to a boil and cook on medium heat for 4 hours, adding sea salt for flavour. Turn off heat, break up meat chunks and remove large bones. Add 3 fingers of brandy, stir and serve!

H.T.'s Tips:

- Add sliced ginseng root to the soup for good for circulation.
- Avoid old chicken. It's too gamey.

What exactly are 3 fingers of brandy?

It is a linear measurement that varies from person to person. Put your first three fingers together horizontally and place outside the bottom of a glass or shot glass. Fill the glass to the height of the 3 fingers. Your 3 fingers together is the linear measurement. The wider the fingers, the larger the amount.

"Wedding Pudding" Dutch Advokaat

Advokat

My greatest wish for the two of you is that through the years your love for each other will so deepen and grow, that years from now you will look back on this day, your wedding day, as the day you loved each other the least.
~ Unknown

In a culture full of in-law jokes, I am proud to say I love and adore my in-laws dearly. Jack and Helen Roorda have been in my life for over twenty years and have never over-stayed their welcome. They raised five children, two refugee teenagers and over twenty foster children. Helen is an extraordinary cook and her dinners are legendary. She makes a great soup with mini meatballs. If you show up in time for a meal, the family will joke that the soup was actually spaghetti and she just added water to make it stretch further.

Helen enjoys making new and interesting dishes and is always looking for unique and obscure ingredients. Every dish she has ever prepared has been absolutely delicious... except for one. Of all the meals she has prepared for her family over the years, there is only one dish that went awry and they never let her live it down. Her family loves her food and they are all adventurous eaters. With a family of constant jokesters, however, the tomato aspic dinner, served over twenty-five years ago, was tough to "stomach" and continues to be something they hold over her just for fun.

Jack Roorda and Helen Idsinga both emigrated from The Netherlands to Canada in 1952 when they were both fourteen years old. Their hometowns were only a couple of miles apart in Friesland, but they never met until their families both settled in the same small town of Clinton, Ontario.

Anyone who emigrated from Europe to Canada in those days came by boat and went through Customs at the harbour in Halifax, Nova Scotia. Jack's Dutch name was Jappie and Helen's birth name was Hiltje. They were both given new English names by family members.

In 1960, Jack and Helen married in their church. Friends and family from all over were invited. They are each the eldest of ten children in their families, so they were not short of "hands" to prepare for the occasion.

Advokaat is a special Dutch treat that was traditionally served at weddings and Christmas. When it is prepared authentically, it is more like a pudding than a drink, though you can buy it as a drink today. Preparing it is a both a science and an art. Traditionally it is served in small fancy glass bowls and eaten with very small Dutch silver spoons.

A devout Baptist woman attended Jack and Helen's wedding and she was strict about not drinking. The Advokaat at their wedding was made by Helen's mom and sisters. It was especially creamy and delicious. When the Baptist woman tasted the "pudding" she happily went back for second and third helpings, not knowing it was spiked. No one knows if she figured it out, but she got tipsy enough for it to be chuckled over many years later.

This summer, Jack and Helen gathered the whole family together to celebrate their 50th wedding anniversary. They rented a large chalet to host their brood of twenty-two that included children, spouses, grandchildren and their special great-granddaughter. It was a time of great fun and great food!

"Wedding Pudding" Dutch Advokaat

Serves 6

Ingredients:

10 egg yolks
1/2 teaspoon salt
1 1/3 cups sugar
1 1/2 cups brandy or gin
2 teaspoons vanilla extract

1. In a mixer, beat the egg yolks, salt and sugar until they thicken. Pour the brandy in slowly and continue beating.

2. Pour the mixture in a saucepan and warm it up over a low heat. Whisk the mixture continuously to keep the consistency smooth while it cooks and thickens. Do not let it boil as the alcohol will evaporate.

3. It is ready when the mixture coats the back of a spoon. Take it off the heat and whisk the vanilla extract into it.

4. Allow to cool. Serve in cocktail glasses and garnish with whipped cream. Traditional Dutch Advokaat is thick and eaten with dessert spoons.

5. Store in the refrigerator.

"Eet Smakelijk"

Advokaat

ZEELAND

"Nightmare Kitchen" Chicken with Sun-dried Tomatoes and Cream

chicken

A glass for the vodka, for the beer a mug, and for the table, cheerful company.
~ Russian proverb

by Chef Janet

The air was hot, the food was hot and so was I. I was not happy cooking in this tiny, tiny kitchen on the hottest summer night! It was August, the air was still sweltering at 4 p.m. and I was cooking for free.

A year earlier, at a charity function, four women had won a gift certificate for a free dinner, but when we tried to set a date, they kept changing their plans. Realizing they were all single, I suggested a more informal buffet for eight. One of them had a twenty-year old daughter who had taken some food courses, so they volunteered her to be my helper.

I arrived and... there were now ten women! I told myself it was not a big problem and got my "volunteer" busy making fancy martinis and blender drinks. She was doing a great job. Then as the evening progressed, it got hotter and hotter and my young volunteer got very drunk and finally passed out! Can you see where this is going?

If that wasn't bad enough, there were the dogs - ten dogs! Yes. Ten. Each woman had brought her dog, so every time I turned around there was a dog underfoot eating the garbage or trying to chew skewers from appetizers. And because it was so wickedly hot, the owners took turns coming into the kitchen to get glasses of water for their dogs. Wonder why these women are single? "Geez!" I thought, "I'm going to kill someone!"

If that wasn't distraction enough, there was a tenant from Japan whom I had thrown out of my nightmare kitchen at least twenty times. In the middle of the evening she came in again and said, "Chef, excuse, please?" I turned around and 'SNAP.' She took my picture! "Oh, I send picture to Japan!" she tells me. Can you imagine what that picture says? My face was beet red and glowing under my white hat!

Toward the end of the evening, my volunteer sobered up and came into the kitchen with something on her mind. "Can I tell you something, but don't tell my Mum?"

"Is she pregnant?" I immediately thought, "No. I do not want to know!"

She was not pregnant. Instead, her five foot boa constrictor had gotten lost in the house that evening while she was unconscious. She couldn't find it and both her Mum and the tenant were petrified of it. Do you blame them?

That night, as I packed the car, I decided that I had to laugh! Laughter and tears can be so similar. Tired and exhausted, I unpacked only some of my things before heading to bed. The next morning, as I went out to unload the rest my stuff the thought suddenly occurred to me. "What if the joke is on me? What if I have the snake?!"

1,5 oz
1oz

"Nightmare Kitchen" Chicken with Sun-Dried Tomatoes and Cream

Serves 8

Ingredients:

6 boneless skinless chicken breasts (cooked and chopped)
3 sweet peppers (red, orange or yellow) chopped
1 bag sun-dried tomatoes (chopped) oil packed is fine
20 mushrooms
6-8 shallots chopped
4-5 tablespoons butter
2 1/2 cups chicken broth
1 cup vodka
1 tablespoon fresh dill
1 tablespoon fresh thyme
Salt/pepper
4/5 cup whipping cream

1. Chop all veggies and sauté in 3 tablespoons butter.

2. Add sun-dried tomatoes, chicken and spices. Adjust them to taste. Sauté until flavours are well combined. About 4 minutes.

3. Add vodka, steam for 1 minute and then add broth.

4. Simmer for 1 hour. Continue to season to taste. Should have a distinct dill and vodka flavour.

5. Add whipping cream just before serving.

6. Sauce should still be quite runny!

Serve in bowls with fresh crusty bread.

Find out more about Chef Janet at www.CookingWithSin.com.

"Perfect First Date" Mojito Leg of Lamb

Mojito Lamb

I pity them greatly, but I must be mum,
for how could we do without sugar and rum?
~ William Cowper

by Heather Jurczyk

We generally don't tell this story when people ask how Jeff and I met. Most of the time people give us these crazy blank stares of, "You did what? Seriously?" We stick to 'met through friends'. 'Friends' is basically the Internet and 'met' is pretty much we Twittered each other to death. We just had too much in common. Both food bloggers? Check. Both computer geeks? Check. Both made a silly decision to bake our way through a virtual bread bible? Checkity check check. So when I casually mentioned to Jeff that I was moving back home to the Midwest and driving myself thousands of miles across the US, he simply said, "Want company?"

And in truth, that was how we met met. Face to face. On the roof of an airport parking garage in the middle of Nowhere, New Mexico. I must have thought, "Hey! We don't really know each other. Why not drive along together in a cramped vehicle for umpteen million hours and abuse our bodies with energy drinks and beef jerky and chex mix and cheddarwursts and gummie bears? Because that my friends, is the perfect idea for a first date!" Apparently, Jeff concurred.

Actually, it was what happened afterwards that made it all worthwhile. You can call it 'kitchen magic'. We ate. Oh did we eat. And we cooked, and grilled, and baked, smoked, roasted, fried, sautéed and more. I cooked for Jeff and Jeff cooked for me. We cooked together and nearly killed each other in the process. But somewhere between, "I think I know how to chop an onion!" and, "No kidding? That's bacon? I thought it was a puppy," the smoke from the kitchen fire cleared and we realized just how darn good we were together.

RUM
SACCHARUM
OFFICINARUM
750ml
40%
ALC/VOL
DISTILLING PERFECTION
FROM FIRST PRESS
CANE

"Perfect First Date" Mojito Leg of Lamb

Serves 6

Ingredients:

5 lb. leg of lamb, bone in
3/4 cup light rum
3/4 cup fresh mint (spearmint)
3/4 cup fresh squeezed lime juice
1/3 cup sugar
2 habanero peppers
6 cloves garlic
1 large white onion, roughly chopped
1 1/2 tablespoons cumin
1/2 teaspoon salt
1/2 teaspoon pepper
3 tablespoons vegetable oil

1. Combine all ingredients, except lamb, in a food processor and pulse to combine.

2. Pour over lamb and allow it to marinade for 24 hours, turning occasionally. (8 hours or less is fine for chicken.)

3. Grill until done, basting occasionally with the marinade. A 5 lb. leg of lamb generally takes about 2 hours; your meat thermometer will read 145ºF for medium rare (preferred), and 160ºF for medium to medium well.

Heather and Jeff serve it with Lemon Onion Israeli Couscous and Touch O'Mint Tzatziki.

Find out more about Heather & Jeff at www.CookingWithSin.com.

Lemon Onion Israeli Couscous

Ingredients:

1 cup Israeli couscous
2 tablespoons olive oil
1 yellow onion, cut into eighths
2 cups chicken broth or water
1 tablespoon fresh chopped parsley
juice of one lemon
1 teaspoon red pepper flakes
salt and pepper to taste

1. Toast couscous in olive oil for about 5 minutes, until golden.

2. Add in the onions and sauté till just translucent.

3. Add broth/water and bring to a boil. Reduce heat and let simmer until almost all the broth is gone and the couscous is tender, about 10 minutes or so.

4. Add parsley, pepper flakes, lemon juice, salt and pepper and serve immediately.

Touch O' Mint Tzatziki

Ingredients:

1 cup plain Greek yogurt, drained.
1 cucumber, peeled, seeded, grated and drained.
3 cloves garlic - minced
1 tablespoon white wine vinegar
squeeze of half a lime
1 tablespoon fresh dill
1 teaspoon fresh chopped mint
1 teaspoon salt
fresh ground pepper to taste
1-2 tablespoons extra virgin olive oil

1. Combine all ingredients except the olive oil. Refrigerate till ready to serve.

2. Immediately before serving, add 1-2 tablespoon of olive oil and mix to blend well.

"Sisterhood" Maple Rum Crêpes

maple crêpes

I know my older sister loves me because she gives me all her old clothes and has to go out and buy new ones.
~ Lauren, 4 years old

by Darcelle Runciman

This delicious dessert has been in our family for years. Originally handed down by my sister, Nicole, she created this work of art one day, and we all fell in love with making crêpes from that moment on. We knew we needed to get the recipe. When we asked she delivered.

With a few minor changes over the years, and the addition of using the crêpes for different meals, it is now a part of our family tradition. My fifteen year-old stepson loves eating and making these crêpes on his own (minus the "sin"), as a fun creative dish for breakfast. He has even added blueberries, and sometimes chocolate to his creations.

Speaking of love, my husband Pat and I met ten years ago and our love of the outdoors and of cooking is part of what brought us together. One of our first trips together outside Canada was to the Dominican Republic. I remember we ate at a local café and enjoyed chocolate crêpes. Now, having this recipe, we carry on that tradition. We love the outdoors so much that we were married on a beautiful sand beach in Prince Edward County in Ontario. We love spending time in the kitchen creating good food for family and friends. It's been five years since we were married, and we'll be celebrating my sister's wedding this year. You can bet crêpes will be on our breakfast menu!

I remember one day just before lunch when I was visiting my sister and we both did not feel like cooking. We looked at each other and decided to go to our local breakfast restaurant to have – crêpes, of course! I love that we can share laughs and food and create moments in time that we remember forever.

Our family is very close. We love getting together and enjoying each other's time and cooking and having fun in the kitchen. It is simply part of what we do, and something I believe that has been handed down by our grandmother who was always in the kitchen. My sister and I love baking and she now owns her own cupcake business, and has won awards for her unique displays of "sinful" treats.

Having lived in Montreal for twenty-one of my years there are many French inspired dishes that were created by my sister and myself over time. The crêpe is one of my favourites. The love that goes into creating these masterpieces will tickle your taste buds and have you coming back for more. Enjoy!

Read more from Darcelle's post at www.CookingWithSin.com where she shares the history of the crêpe and more details of her story.

"Sisterhood" Maple Rum Temptation Crêpes

Serves 4

These delicious crêpes can be used for dessert, breakfast or main course. This *sin*ful treat comes with an impressive sauce.

Crêpes

Ingredients:

3 eggs
1 1/3 cup 2% milk
1 teaspoon vanilla
3/4 cup flour
1/8 teaspoon salt
1/4 cup butter, melted

1. Mix eggs with milk and vanilla and set aside.
2. In a large separate bowl, mix the flour and salt. Add egg mixture to the flour and salt mixture and mix well with a whisk.
3. Once all ingredients are mixed without lumps, melt butter.
4. Add butter slowly to mixture, beating continuously.
5. Grease pan (a pan the size of the crêpe you want) with oil or cooking spray. Once heated, use a large cooking spoon to put 2 scoops of crêpe mixture in pan so that crêpes are thin. Flip once and set aside. Best served warm.

Maple Rum Sauce

Ingredients:

1/2 cup quality maple syrup
1/3 cup whipping cream
1/3 cup butter
3 tablespoons dark rum

1. Combine first 3 ingredients in a small saucepan on medium. Heat and stir until butter is melted and mixture is boiling.
2. Boil gently for about 3 minutes, stirring occasionally, until thickened. Add rum and stir. Makes about 1 cup (250ml) of sauce.

Toppings:

Add fruit just prior to serving to crêpes. Bananas, raspberries, strawberries, blueberries and blackberries work well. Top with whipped cream and Maple Rum Sauce.

"Just Like Gold" Jamaican Rum Cake

Rum cake

The chief fuddling they make in the island is Rumbullion, alias Kill-Divil, and this is made of sugar canes distilled, a hot, hellish, and terrible liquor.
~ 1651 Caribbean document

Adam Hewson's mother Claudette would make up a large jar of "fruit" every year. She would mix together raisins, currants, citrus peel and other dried fruit and let it sit for months soaking in rum. He remembers it being a large 5L mason jar that he loved and admired. He says that jar of fruit was like gold to him.

Claudette loved cooking all types of interesting foods and baking all kinds of delicious sweets. Her heritage was Jamaican and her rum cake was a very special treat, but she liked to try foods from all over the world. It was in this world of wonderful foods that Adam was raised and he has carried on Claudette's love of cooking. Adam is quiet and easy-going, but if you sit down and talk to him about cooking, he comes alive. He loves to try different food combinations and use the freshest and most authentic ingredients.

Right now, Adam has 5 jars of fruit at home. He mixed them up months ago and hasn't decided yet when he will use them. Some people will put some wine in too, but Adam says it's best with white overproof rum alone.

Adam will make up a jar of fruit any time of the year. He may try to time it for Christmas, but he may leave it sit for a year or more. Once he had let a jar sit for 3 years and he knew he had gold on his hands. Just for fun he told his cousin, a professional chef, that he thought it might not be good anymore and was thinking of throwing it out. His cousin gulped and begged to take it off his hands. Adam wisely declined.

White
ERPROOF RUM
LTD
750 ml

"Just Like Gold" Jamaican Rum Cake

Step 1: The Fruit

Ingredients:

1 cup raisins
1/2 cup prunes, chopped into small pieces
1/2 cup currants
1/2 cup mixed fruit peel
1 bottle white overproof rum (63% alc./vol.)
1 2-cup mason jar with lid

1. Mix the fruit and put it into the jar. Add the rum and give the fruit-rum mix a good stir and put the lid on tight.

2. Shake the jar to make sure the fruit is all covered in the liquid. There should be a little room left at the top of the jar so you can turn it occasionally to stir the fruit. You may even want to turn the jar upside down for a while.

3. Let the fruit sit for 3 weeks to 3 years. It's your choice!

4. Extra rum is needed over time. As the fruit absorbs the rum, you will need to add more to keep the fruit covered.

Adam's Tip:

If you want to make a larger batch, the proportions are 2 cups fruit to 1 cup rum.

Curious about which rum Adam uses?
Find out on his post at www.CookingWithSin.com.
Plus, learn the Jamaican rhyme for Rum Punch.

"Just Like Gold" Jamaican Rum Cake

Step 2: The Cake

Ingredients:

3 cups brown sugar
1 cup butter, softened at room temperature
6 eggs
1 teaspoon real vanilla
2 cups flour
1/4 teaspoon cinnamon
1/4 teaspoon grated fresh nutmeg
3 teaspoon baking powder
The 2 1/2 cups of the fruit mix

1. Preheat the oven to 300ºF. Grease a 9 inch spring form pan and line the bottom and the corners with parchment. Lightly dust the sides with flour.

2. Cream butter and sugar.

3. Blend in eggs and vanilla.

4. Add flour, sugar, spices, salt, pepper & baking powder mixing on medium speed.

5. Stir in fruit by hand until consistent. Drain off some of the fruit juices before to get the a nice consistency. Save the extra juices to top up other fruit mixtures.

6. Bake in a spring form pan for 2 hours at 300ºF.

7. Cool pan on a baking rack.

Jamaican Rum Cake can be served iced or plain with a brandy sauce drizzled over it, but Adam prefers to serve his plain. He feels the icing and sauce take away from the simplicity of the recipe and may dominate the key ingredient, the rum fruit.

It is distinctly smooth and rich. The cake can be stored wrapped at room temperature for a long time to let the rum ripen the flavours further. You can brush on more rum to richen it over time.

"We are Family" Whisky Brie and Whisky Fondue (plus Sweet Rye Bread)

Whisky Brie

What whisky will not cure, there is no cure for.
~ An Irish Proverb

When it comes to family it may be true that "blood is thicker than water," but I know that water can be turned into blood.

My Johnson family has a long and very close connection with the Phibbs family. Growing up together, the connections were so tightly interwoven the adults were all called "aunt" and "uncle" and us kids thought of each other as cousins, though there is no blood relationship.

My Johnson grandparents were raising their young family during the depression when they first connected with the Phibbs family on the Canadian prairies. The two families quickly became close and, along with extended family members, decided to migrate east together. The journey took several days and was quite an adventure: 22 people, one cube van, one car, the flat tires, the furniture precariously balanced on trailers, the active kids.

With so many bodies packed in tightly, one of the young adults thought he would be more comfortable travelling in the trailer carrying the mattresses. (These were the days long before seat belts!) At one point the trailer came unhitched and he had to deal with a surprise "trip" of his own.

On route, the group stopped to visit relatives in a small town. They parked out on the road and when people passing by saw all the bodies climbing out of the vehicles and trailers, they thought gypsies had arrived. It was the talk of the town.

After a few years of living in the new town, the Phibbs clan packed up their belongings and moved again. Before long, the Johnsons followed and moved in with the Phibbs. It was a zoo until my grandparents found a place of their own. Both our families' roots were finally put down and they stayed.

Several Johnson and Phibbs family members don't drink alcohol, so when one of the aunts heard about this project, she sent a recipe for Rye Bread. Rye the grain, that is, because Canadian whisky is made with rye and often called "Rye." It was a very sweet mix-up of words.

A couple heard about the rye bread and shared their Whisky Brie and Whisky Cheese Fondue recipes. They don't drink liquor, but had won a bottle of whisky as a door prize and didn't know what to do with it. They didn't want to give it away, because that would encourage someone else to "sin", but they thought it would be a waste to throw it out. They had an "a-ha" moment during a hockey party. They tried adding it to their favourite cheese appetizers. Cooking, they knew would burn the alcohol off. Their friends loved it! Cooking with the "sin" was the best solution for them.

The Johnsons and the Phibbs have a very special relationship that is as rich and solid as family. The families have been close friends for 72 years... and counting. Interestingly though, there has never been a marriage between the two families – probably because we thought we were related!

Whisky Brie

"We Are Family" Rye Bread

Ingredients:

1 package dry yeast
2 cups milk, scalded
1/2 teaspoon salt
1/4 cup white sugar
1/2 cup brown sugar
1 teaspoon anise seed
1/4 cup molasses
1 1/2 teaspoons lemon juice
1/4 cup shortening, melted
1 cup dark rye flour
4 cups all-purpose flour

1. Dissolve the yeast in warm water.

2. Transfer the scalded milk to a large bowl, and add the salt, white sugar, brown sugar, anise seed, molasses, lemon juice and melted shortening. Stir and let the mixture cool to lukewarm.

3. Once the mixture is lukewarm add the dissolved yeast.

4. Add the rye flour, beating it with mixer. Gradually beat in the white flour, kneeding the last cup or two by hand on a floured surface.

5. Place the dough in a greased bowl, and turn to coat the surface. Cover it with a damp towel, and allow to rise in a warm place for about 1 1/2 hours until it doubles in size.

6. Punch down the dough, and place it on a lightly floured surface. Knead it well until it becomes elastic and separate the dough into 3 loaves.

7. Place in greased 9 x 5 inch bread pans. Let rise in the pans for 3/4 of an hour or more, then bake at 325ºF for an hour.

Note: The dough is absolutely delicious, so keep your sampling to a minimum, otherwise you may only have enough for 2 loaves.

"We Are Family" Whisky Brie

Ingredients:

1 226 g (8 oz.) wheel of Brie cheese
1/4 cup brown sugar
1/4 cup chopped pecans
1/4 cup whisky

1. Preheat the oven to 350ºF (175ºC).

2. Make 1/4 inch deep crisscross cuts on the top of the Brie wheel. Place the Brie in a baking dish with sides. Warm the Brie in the preheated oven until it is softened, about 5 minutes.

3. While it is warming, stir together the brown sugar, pecans and rye whisky in a small bowl.

4. Pour the mix on top of the warmed wheel of Brie, making sure it goes into the slits and return it to the oven for another 10 minutes.

5. Serve it warm in the the dish. Use a spoon to scoop the cheese onto crackers or baguette.

"We Are Family" Whisky Fondue

Ingredients:

1 large sweet onion, minced
1 tablespoon butter
1 cup milk
1 pound (450 g) grated extra-sharp cheddar cheese
1 tablespoon cornstarch
1/3 cup whisky
1 loaf marble rye bread, cubed for dipping

1. In a heavy saucepan, gently sauté the onions in the butter until caramelized, clear but not browned.

2. Add milk and bring to a simmer. Stir in cheddar cheese until melted.

3. Purée the mixture until smooth then transfer back to the saucepan.

4. Whisk together cornstarch and whisky until smooth. While constantly stirring, slowly pour whisky mixture into cheese mixture and continue to cook until thickened.

5. Pour cheddar whisky fondue into a fondue pot or heat-proof bowl. Serve with marble rye bread as dippers.

"Working Past Midnight" French Toast

French Toast

To be or not to be cointreauversial, that is the question.
~ with apologies to William Shakespeare (From the Cointreau website)

Some people have a natural ability to see new possibilities and Margaret and Robert Campbell are the best. After years working in careers, running businesses and counting down to retirement, they could have chosen to rest on their laurels and slow down. But, no! They decided to start a new business.

Each week Margaret and Bob go full tilt. They will attend at least one trade show a week, often travelling a distance, and return to put in long hours running their growing business. They are contemplating starting yet another initiative to build on their business. They go at a pace that would exhaust many people half their age.

Talk to Margaret about food and she bursts with enthusiasm. With such a hectic pace, they value time spent together at home and Margaret makes sure they eat very, very well. She says it usually takes one special ingredient to take a dish from delicious to spectacular. Her beef stroganoff has always been a favourite, but recently she substituted cream cheese for the cream and that put it in a whole new league. There are a couple of kicker ingredients in her French toast recipe: the Cointreau and the cream. It is her favourite thing to serve to guests.

Midnight is the moment where you are ending one day and starting a new one. Bob and Margaret have enthusiasm, and creativity and are always looking to start something new.

"Working Past Midnight" French Toast

Serves 6

Ingredients:

1 dozen eggs
1/2 cup whipping cream
1/2 teaspoon vanilla
Zest of one orange
2 tablespoons Cointreau
1 loaf French bread, cut into 1 inch thick slices

1. Whip together the eggs, cream, vanilla, zest and Cointreau in a large bowl.
2. Place the bread slices in one or more cake pans and pour the egg mixture over all the slices making sure each slice is evenly coated.
3. Cover the pan(s) with a lid or plastic wrap and let sit. It can sit on the counter for 15 minutes or be placed in the fridge overnight.
4. Place the slices on a greased cookie sheet. Bake at 375ºF for 20 to 25 minutes.
5. Serve warm. Can be topped with fresh fruit, whipped cream, or maple syrup.

Garnish Tip:

Peel a slim strip of orange peel and wrap it around a toothpick. Later, pull the toothpick out and the orange peel should be curled and a perfect garnish for your French toast or a beverage.

COINTREAU

"Edible Magic" Scallop Martini

Scallop Martini

If it wasn't for the olives in his martinis, he'd starve to death!
~ Milton Berle

La scoperta di un piatto nuovo pipreziosa per il genere umano che la scoperta di una nuova stella. (The discovery of a new dish is more precious to human beings than the discovery of a new star.)
~ J. A. Brillat-Savarin

It was the annual Wine Pairing Gala, an invitation-only dinner that has been held over the last five years. It was in grand style on this evening that "Chef D" Chef Darryl Fletcher was the host for the gourmet six-course wine and food pairing dinner.

Each course was a unique and special plate that Chef D had prepared using only the finest ingredients with exquisite presentation. Just before each course was served he would come out and describe the dish to the guests. Then, he was followed by the wine importer to share the complexities of the wine that was being paired with each course.

The evening started with teasing the diners' palates with a mouth-watering amuse-bouche that was greeted warmly with a wine that paired perfectly. The next course brought forward, a spring pea soup, took everyone by surprise with its light fresh flavour whose taste only reached a crescendo with the subtle grape essence that slipped past your taste buds with a lover's touch. These diners were excited. These diners were curious. These diners were stoked. Then the atmosphere took a dramatic turn.

There are a few things that distinguish a chef from a common cook. Chefs know food on an intuitive level and can vision combinations that no one has thought of before. Those combinations often test the limits of the most adventurous palates.

When Chef D came out to present the Scallop Martini course, he was excited. It was a whole new dish presented in a whole new way and he knew it was a winner. He began by describing how he seared the large fresh scallops in butter. Then he explained how he prepared the sauce by reducing a mixture of cream and Irish cream. It was at this point that the crowd held their tongues. They listened politely as Chef D finished the description. It was both a tantalizing flavour and a tantalizing experience. The wine maker came up and described what delightful tastes would compliment this unique oral experience to a less than silent crowd. The wine was poured. The wine was swirled and smelt in the glass. As the scallop martini was placed in front of the hesitant guests, soft murmurs of, "I'm not eating that," "Why would you ruin a scallop like that?" and "Why would you ruin Irish cream like that?" were heard around the room.

Slowly the murmurs were replaced with moans of pleasure as the scallops disappeared from the glass in front of each delighted diner. Questions of doubt were replaced with questions as to whether it is polite to drink the sauce out of the bottom of the glass dish. I would be lying if I didn't share that, yes, some licked the glass clean. Everyone in the room was pleasantly amazed and delectably surprised.

Chef D's wife Tric calls his artistry 'Edible Magic' for many good reasons. That night his magic melted a cautious, reluctant crowd into a room of smiling, delighted diners.

Scallop Martini

“Edible Magic” Scallop Martini

Serves 4

Ingredients:

8 large dry scallops
2 tablespoons butter
1 cup 35% cream
1 cup Irish Cream
4 fresh basil leaves

1. In a medium size saucepan, combine the Irish Cream and the 35% cream. On medium heat, let it boil until it reduces by 3/4 stirring occasionally. It will become thick. This should take about 12 to 15 minutes. Make sure mixture does not boil over.

2. Once mixture reduces, take heat down to a simmer.

3. In a large non-stick fry pan (or cast iron) over high heat, warm up the pan for about 2 minutes, add butter and let it melt before adding scallops. Cook scallops 1 1/2 minutes on each side.

4. Place 2 scallops in each Martini glass. Drizzle the cream sauce over top and garnish with fresh basil.

Find out more about Chef D at www.CookingWithSin.com.

Milk and Cookies for the "Real" Santa

Milk and Cookies

Someone is putting brandy in your bonbons, Grand Marnier in your breakfast jam, Kahlua in your ice cream, Scotch in your mustard and Wild Turkey in your cake.
~ Marian Burros

It took a year of hanging out, just having fun together and dating other people for both Marc Hoare and Jenn Burr to realize they didn't want to go on without each other. When they celebrated their wedding, they did it up in true style. An elegant historic hotel, Jenn's perfect white dress and the gorgeous decorations made the day a truly special event. Their families and close friends all came together, happy to celebrate the union of such a uniquely special couple.

Just as you would expect, they wrote their vows with a lot of thought and consideration. But these two love a good laugh and are full of adventure. At the end of her vows, when Jenn told Marc, "You are the cheese on my cracker," everyone roared! That phrase put their wedding on the map!

Marc and his friends are well known for their antics. They can find fun pretty much anywhere and at any time. One Christmas, he was spending time with his cousins. After dinner, dessert came out. To his delight, this particular dessert proved to be amazing. It was layers of cookies and milk with Kahlua and whipped cream and chocolate. Between the Kahlua in the dessert and the alcohol in their glasses, the jokes began to roll. They all thought it was hilarious that someone had made a dessert out of milk and cookies at Christmas time. Adding Kahlua was a great twist on the traditional fare set out for Santa each year. Throughout the discussion and laughter, guys who had played Santa in the past wondered, "Where were these milk and cookies at the time we used to put gifts out?" No one really remembers what the original name of the dessert was, but that night Marc and his cousins renamed it Milk and Cookies for the 'Real' Santa! It is an annual favourite.

Milk and Cookies for the “Real” Santa

Serves 8

Ingredients:

1/2 cup Kahlua
1/2 cup milk
350 g (12 oz.) package of chocolate chip cookies
4 cups whipped dessert topping
2 chocolate & toffee bars, crushed

1. Soak cookies in a mixture of Kahlua and milk for about a minute. Don’t let them soak through or they will be too soggy.

2. Place half of the soaked cookies in an 8x 8” cake pan, covering the whole bottom.

3. Spread half of the whipped topping over the cookies creating approximately a 1” layer.

4. Repeat process to make another layer of cookies and whipped topping.

5. Crush up the chocolate & toffee bars into fine pieces and spread over the top. Top with chocolate chips, shaved chocolate or anything else that inspires you!

6. Place it in the freezer for 3 - 4 hours and serve.

Marc’s Tip:

Store bought cookies work really well, but you can make it with homemade cookies if you wish.

Have fun with the links on Marc & Jenn’s post at www.CookingWithSin.com.

"Mountain Top" Trebević Cake

Trebević Cake

Climb the mountains and get their good tidings. Nature's peace will flow into you as sunshine flows into trees. The winds will blow their own freshness into you, and the storms their energy, while cares will drop off like autumn leaves.
~ John Muir

If you have ever stood on a mountain peak, you know how the stunning view can give you a new perspective on life. The world below with its miniature houses and trees seems simple and serene. From the mountain top, the world always looks completely at peace.

Valentina grew up in Sarajevo with Mount Trebević watching over the city. Sarajevo is protected on all sides by seven mountains and Trebević is the smallest and closest. Val remembers how easy it was to take the street car to the gondola and enjoy a fun day up on the mountain. In 1984, this small mountain hosted the Olympic bobsleigh run and it was on the top of Trebević with the breathtaking views, that Val said "I do" to Radomir, the love of her life.

Val grew up in a home full of joy, family and friends. Her mother was always baking something special for her and her friends. Her parents treated her friends just like family.

One of the favourite cakes Val's mom baked was called "Trebević," named after their dear mountain. It was a favourite at any event because it was a cake you could "dress up" or "dress down." Her mom would use premium chocolate and high end ingredients for special occasions and less expensive chocolate if it was going to be gobbled up by a pack of hungry children.

After their marriage, Valentina worked with Radomir building their new home. It took three years and when they finally moved in, Val's mom passed on to her a copy of the recipe for "Trebević." It had been a special part of Val's childhood and she looked forward to sharing it with her own children.

It was 1992. Val and Rad had only been in their new home for eight months when the political tensions in Sarajevo intensified. Val was two months pregnant and the hospital for new babies had been destroyed, so she and Rad decided to go to Belgrade for a few days and wait for clearer political heads to prevail.

To avoid suspicion they packed up a small bag of things for a day trip: a few items of clothing and some toiletries. They planned to return soon and left everything else behind, including the Trebević recipe. Valentina and Radomir never returned to their home.

Ultimately all of their family and most of their friends had to leave Sarajevo to start new lives scattered all over the world. Val and Rad eventually chose Canada as their new home.

In the early nineties it was difficult to find and reconnect with old friends. The web and email were very new and social networking was unheard of. While Val embraced life in her new homeland, she missed her friends and worked hard to track them down.

One of Val's dearest friends was found living in Vienna and they were thrilled to find each other. Her friend had also left with virtually nothing and faced the same struggle starting life in a new country. They enjoyed exchanging letters.

One of her friend's letters mentioned that she had especially thought of Val and her mother because she baked Trebević that day. Val was wonderfully surprised! Somehow, even in her haste to leave, her friend had managed to save the recipe.

The friend sent a copy of the recipe and once again it was back in Val's family. Not only was she pleased to have her mom's recipe back, but she was also pleased to have a memento of the beautiful mountain under whose shelter she had grown up.

Trebević Cake

"Mountain Top" Trebević Cake

Cake

1 1/2 cups sugar
3 eggs
1 1/2 cup chopped pecans
2 cups grated or puréed apple (4-5 apples)
2/3 cup vegetable oil
1 tablespoon baking powder
4 tablespoons cocoa powder
1 cup flour
3 ounces hazelnut liqueur

1. Preheat the oven to 400ºF. Grease a 9 x 13 cake pan.

2. Beat the sugar and eggs together well with a mixer. Use a large bowl. Stirring by hand, add all the rest of the ingredients into the sugar-egg mix.

3. Pour the batter into the cake pan and bake for 30 minutes.

"Glazura" Icing

2 eggs
2 cups white sugar (NOT icing sugar)
1 cup chocolate chips
1 ounce of hazelnut liqueur
1 1/4 cups butter, softened to room temperature

1. Beat the eggs and sugar together well with a mixer, then place the mix in the microwave for approximately 2 minutes to thicken it. Stir it regularly to check.

2. While the mix is still hot, stir in the chocolate chips and liqueur until the chocolate melts throughout and is stirred evenly throughout the mix. Using a mixer, beat the butter into the egg/sugar/chocolate mix until fluffy.

4. Put the icing on the cake while the cake is still warm from the oven. Turn the oven off, then return the newly iced cake back to the oven for 10 minutes. With the oven off, the top of the icing will harden while the rest of the cake retains its rich moisture.

Note: While there are a lot of apples in this cake, it does not taste like an apple cake, so spices that work well with apples often don't work well with this recipe. Treat this cake as you would chocolate brownies. Just like Valentina's mom, you can make if for special occasions and use high-end ingredients and better quality chocolate or you can make it for a casual gathering and use less expensive ingredients. It works for every event.

"Today is your day! Your mountain is waiting. So... get on your way."
~ Dr. Seuss

Trebevic Cake

"Shes a Trooper" Cherries Jubilee

cherries

I feel the end approaching. Quick, bring me my dessert, coffee and liqueur.
~ Pierette, great-aunt of Anthelme Brillat-Savarin

Health, strength and endurance are essential to living a vibrant life and taking good care of herself is something Sally Vlaar values deeply. She starts every day with a good one hour walk and she'll jump at any chance to get in a good run, too.

Her strength and endurance have served her very well. A few years ago, Sally was doing home care work travelling from house to house attending to the needs of people confined to their homes. Sally was visiting one particular house on an icy winter day when she slipped and fell hard onto the concrete sidewalk. The pain in her foot seared through her body. She knew she was in big trouble when she reached for her ankle and found it snapped over at a disturbingly unnatural angle.

At the time, cell phones were not attached to everyone, like they are today. Sally knew she had to get herself to a phone. Not wanting to yell and disturb the bed-ridden person in the home, she pulled herself onto her knees. Careful to protect her badly broken ankle, she crawled back to the house, up the front stairs and let herself in the door. Keeping her composure, and not wanting to alarm the homeowner, she called out and identified herself as she made her way to the phone.

At this point, even the strongest among us would have collapsed and called 911. Not Sally. Her son-in-law Darcy says, "She's a trooper," and he is so right. Worried more about the people under her care than her own ankle, the first call she made was to her dispatcher at work, to let them know she couldn't make the rest of her rounds. Then she called her husband to pick her up and take her to the hospital. She could have called 911, but she believed there were worse emergencies at that moment than her ankle and didn't want to occupy an ambulance unnecessarily.

A few months ago, she was hospitalized for several days with a serious health concern. Even in her weakened state with all kinds of tubes and vials connected to her, she got out of the bed several times a day and walked the hospital halls dragging the pole with her.

Since that hospital stay, she has had to change her already very healthy diet drastically. Fats and alcohol are almost completely cut out now and one thing she misses is her Cherries Jubilee. She loves making it and she loves serving it.

Sally says to make sure you serve it in the evening in dim light so you can enjoy the blue flame. Once she served it to her family in the light of day, but no one could see the flame so she increased the quantity of Kirsch. The flame was huge... and so hot it almost burnt her arm!

This recent health scare forced her to slow down - for a brief stint - but now Sally is back to walking an hour a day and getting in a good run when she can.

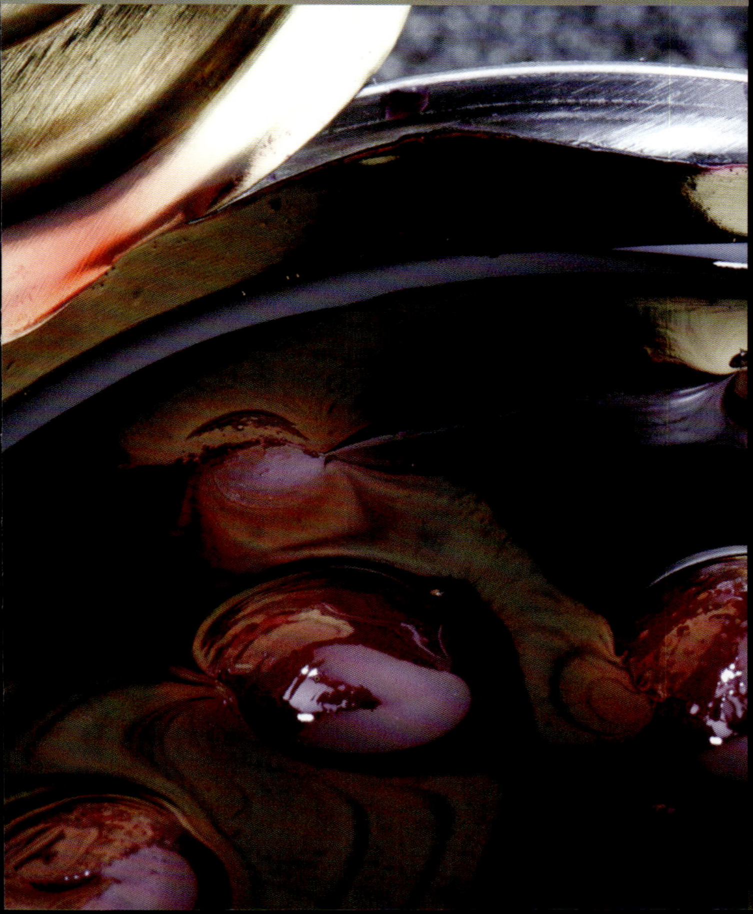

"She's a Trooper" Cherries Jubilee

Serves 4-6

Ingredients:

1 398mL can pitted Bing Cherries
(These are dark cherries, not sour cherries, nor cherry pie filling)
1/4 cup sugar
2 tablespoons cornstarch
1/4 cup Kirsch or a cherry brandy
Vanilla ice cream

Equipment:

1 heavy sauce pan
1 large serving bowl that can handle flames
4 - 6 small serving dishes that can handle flames
1 ladle that can handle flames and has a handle that will keep your hand away from the flames.

1. Mix a small amount of the canned cherry juice with the cornstarch. Makes sure the juice is cold and stir until the cornstarch is blended. It will make a cloudy liquid.

2. Strain the remaining canned cherry juice into a heavy sauce pan, add the sugar and heat on medium-high heat, stirring to dissolve the sugar.

3. Just before the juice and sugar mix comes to a boil, slowly stir in the cornstarch mix, keeping the heat on medium-high. Once the cornstarch is mixed in, let it come to a boil. Keep stirring until the liquid thickens and is clear and shiny.

4. Stir in the cherries and heat until everything is heated through. The cherries can be added earlier with the cornstarch, but the cherries don't need to be cooked.

5. Pour the mix into a nice glass or ceramic serving dish that can that can handle a bit of heat.

6. Scoop the ice cream into individual glass or ceramic bowls that can handle some heat.

7. Pour the kirsch into a ladle that can handle heat and light it. It is best to use a long stick match or a lighter with a long tip and light it just at the edge of the ladle. The flame will travel across quickly, so keep your hand back.

8. Slowly pour the flaming kirsch into the cherry bowl, stirring slowly to let it continue flaming.

9. Pour the cherry mix over the ice cream and enjoy.

The key to flambéing is to shake the cherries gently so the flame continues to burn off some of the harshness of the alcohol and candies the sugars. Your family and guests will be entertained by it, too.

cherries

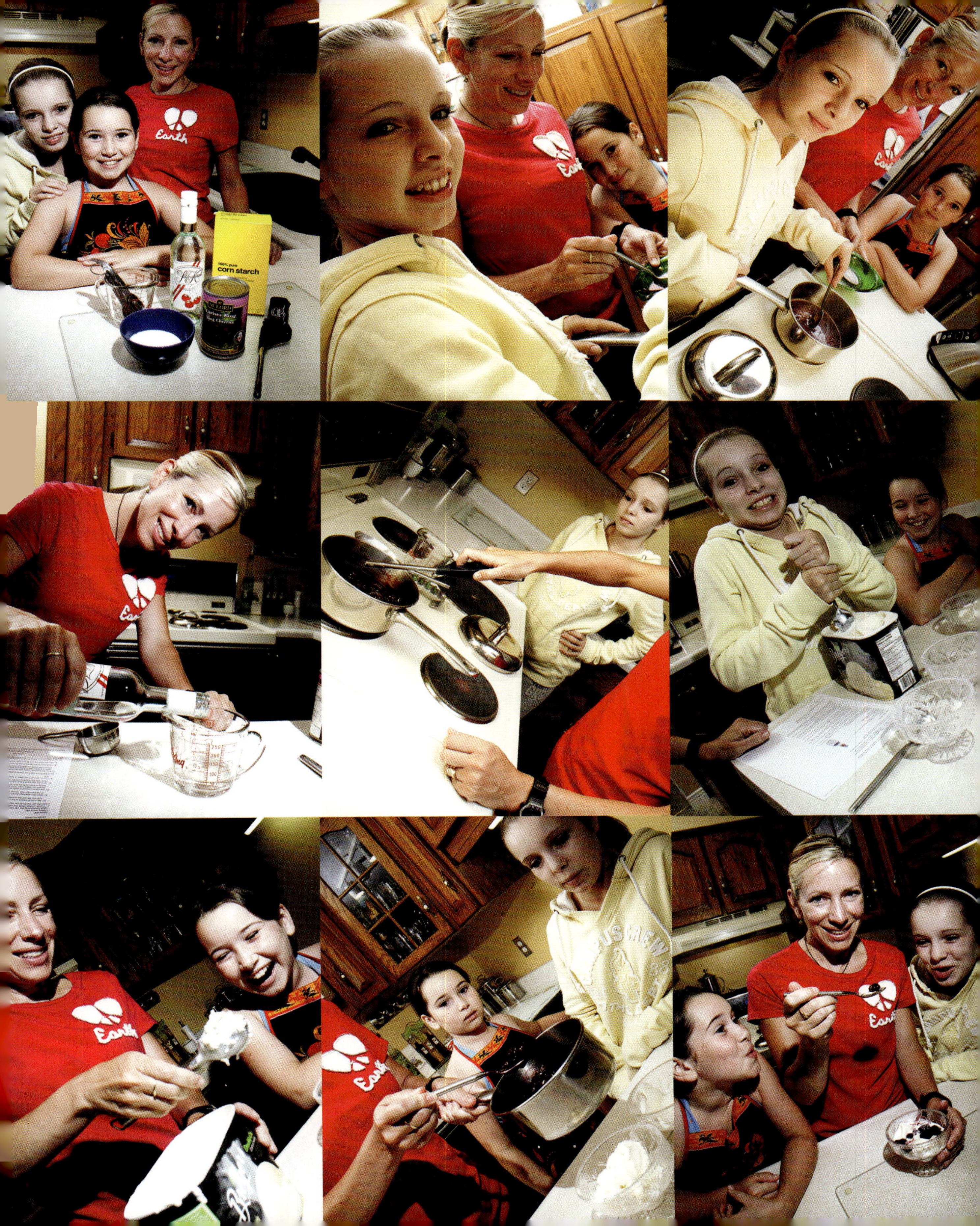
100% pure
corn starch

Sin Supper with the Goddesses

I always love being in the company of women.
It's all about good conversation and great wine.
~ Naomi Watts

God may be in the details, but the goddess is in the questions.
Once we begin to ask them, there's no turning back.
~ Gloria Steinem

Sometimes we call ourselves 'The Goddesses'. Other times we're 'The Divas'. Either way, it's clear what we think of ourselves. We are all teachers or principals who met 10 years ago and though we have all moved on to different schools, we continue to get together a few times a year.

Whatever we have gone through individually, The Goddesses have been there to provide support. We are all passionate about living life vibrantly and with integrity. We all love travel and adventure. We are intellectuals and insist on delving into issues rigorously, especially when it comes to education. Most importantly of all, we laugh loud and we laugh long.

We have seen each other through the inevitable ups and downs of life. Some of us are married, some of us are divorced, some of us have remained single. We raised a glass of bubbly when one of us got married, we poured lots of red wine when one of us faced a break-up and we championed the virtues of being ourselves whether we had a partner or not. We anguished together when some of us faced daunting parenting challenges and we were consoling when some of us faced frustrating health struggles.

After I started my "Cooking With Sin" blog, I decided it would be fun to invite The Goddesses to my house for a "Sin Supper." The jokes ensued. "Can we get tipsy on pork tenderloin?" "I'm bringing a dish called 'Cheddar Cheese Pot' with Riesling, not pot." "We may need to make it a sleep-over."

We had an absolutely wonderful time tasting each other's dishes and ranting about the need for more Arts education in the curriculum. There was Pat's Cheddar Cheese Pot, Laurie's Champagne and Mushroom Chicken and Trish's Pork Tenderloin with Brandied Mushrooms. Gillian brought Pasta de la Coeur and a bottle of Passion-Fruit Jamaican rum. I made George's Sherry Potatoes and Melissa made Better Than Recess for dessert.

I am blessed to have brilliant and creative friends who make an impact on many, many children's lives every day. One of Melissa's students submitted this piece to a writing contest and won. It's a tribute to the work that every teacher around the globe does everyday.

"Ms. Reist has made, and is continuing to make, a huge impact on my life in Grades 5 & 6. She currently teaches Grade 5/6 enrichment at Elizabeth Ziegler PS, a class which I am a part of. Every day, she comes into class full of energy, totally ready, and excited to teach us. It's just so fun to have her as my teacher; she's so vibrant, and always very expressive. I am always as excited as she is to come to class, she really makes it fun! Yes, learning can be fun; I learnt that very quickly with Ms. Reist! She has a certain way of teaching that not only gets across the what, but also the how and the why as well; learning this is so important. Think, how many teachers are like a family friend to you? Mine is."

~ Lucas C. Grade 6

You can read more about our Sin Supper with the Goddesses at www.CookingWithSin.com.

Here are all the recipes from our Sin Supper with the Goddesses one course at a time.

Enjoy!

Cheddar Cheese Pot

Ingredients:

1 lb. hard, sharp cheddar cheese, grated
1 teaspoon mustard powder
1/2 teaspoon nutmeg
1/4 teaspoon cayenne
1/2 cup butter, softened at room temperature
2/3 cup white wine
1/4 cup butter, melted

1. Purée the cheese, mustard powder, nutmeg, cayenne and butter in a food processor until smooth.

2. Add wine slowly, continuing to process the mixture until it is smooth and creamy. Pour it into a serving bowl or pot. Press down to help remove any air pockets.

3. Pour the melted butter over the top and allow butter to set.

4. Serve it with baguette slices or a variety of crackers.

2nd Course:

Champagne and Mushroom Chicken

Step 1: Champagne Chicken

Ingredients:

4 chicken breasts
salt and freshly ground pepper
1 teaspoon fresh chervil
1 teaspoon fresh tarragon
1 teaspoon fresh thyme
1 shallot, quartered
1 cup Champagne (with a sweetness of "1")
4 cups cooked brown rice

1. Place chicken breasts in a broiling pan. Make a slit in each breast and insert a piece of shallot. Season with the salt, pepper and herbs then pour 1/2 cup of the champagne over the breasts.

2. Place the pan under the broiler for 4 minutes until nicely browned. Turn the breasts over and broil the other side for 4 minutes.

3. Remove the chicken from the broiler and place on a baking pan. Spoon the pan juices with the remaining 1/2 cup of Champagne over each breast.

4. Set the oven temperature to 475ºF. Bake the chicken for 30 minutes, basting once or twice.

5. Serve each breast on a bed of cooked rice.

Step 2: Mushroom Sauce

20 small button mushrooms, chopped
1 tablespoon olive oil
1 teaspoon lemon juice
1 teaspoon fresh sage, chopped
1 tablespoon butter

1. Sauté mushrooms in olive oil.

2. Add the lemon juice and sage seasoning to taste. Stir in the butter until it melts.

3. Pour over the chicken and rice and serve.

3rd Course:

Pasta de la Coeur

Ingredients:

1 pound of pasta
3 tablespoons olive oil
1 medium onion, chopped
3 garlic cloves, chopped
6 slices bacon, chopped (not maple-flavoured bacon)
1 cup white wine
1 can (28 ounces) tomato purée
1 teaspoon red pepper flakes, adjust to taste

1. In a large pot of boiling, salted water, cook the pasta until al dente. Drain well. Toss with 1 tablespoon of olive oil and set aside.

2. Cover the bottom of a large pan with 1 tablespoon of olive oil and heat over medium heat.

3. Place the bacon in the pan and fry until it is cooked, but not crispy. Remove the bacon and place it in a dish lined with paper towels to drain. Leave 1 tablespoon of bacon fat in the pan and add 1 tablespoon of olive oil.

4. Sauté the onions in the pan until they are translucent, then add garlic and sauté 1 minute more.

5. Return the bacon to the pan and add the wine. Bring to a boil for 3-4 minutes.

6. Add tomato purée, then use the can and fill it half way with water and add the water to the pan.

7. Add red pepper flakes and simmer on low heat for about 1/2 hour.

8. Serve on the pasta.

4th Course:

Pork Tenderloin with Brandied Mushrooms

Step 1: Pork Tenderloin

3 lbs pork tenderloin
5 cloves of garlic, cut in half
1 teaspoon ground cumin
1 teaspoon sea salt
4 tablespoons soy sauce
2 tablespoons sesame oil
1/2 cup of fig jam or sauce
1/2 cup port

1. Make 10 slits in the tenderloin and insert a 1/2 clove of garlic in each slit.

2. Make a dry mix of the cumin and sea salt and rub down the tenderloin.

3. In a dish, mix the soy sauce, sesame oil, fig jam and port.

4. Pour the mix over the tenderloin, making sure it is fully covered. Marinate the tenderloin for 6 hours or more, turning it over a few times.

5. Cook at 375ºF for 1 1/2 hours. Monitor the cooking time according to the density of the tenderloin. It can be cooked in an open pan or wrapped in foil.

Step 2: Brandied Mushrooms

2 cups cremini mushrooms, sliced
2 shallots, finely cubed
a dash of ground cumin
a dash of sea salt
3/4 cup brandy
1 tablespoon butter
1/2 cup heavy cream

1. In a dish, toss together the mushrooms, shallots, cumin, sea salt and brandy. Stir making sure the mushrooms and shallots are coated evenly. Let it sit for 45 minutes.

2. Warm the butter in a skillet and add the mushroom mix. Simmer on low heat to allow the brandy to reduce slowly.

3. Gently stir in the cream and put in a side dish for serving on the pork tenderloin.

Better Than Recess

Layer 1:

1 cup flour
1/2 cup butter, softened to room temperature
1/2 cup chopped pecans

Mixed together to form the crust base and bake 20 minutes at 350ºF:

Layer 2:

8 oz. cream cheese, softened to room temperature
1 cup icing sugar

Mix cream cheese and icing sugar all together until well blended and smooth. Spread on top of Layer 1 after it has cooled.

Layer 3:

Spread 2 cups of whipped topping over Layer 2.

Layer 4:

Mix:
1 large package of instant chocolate pudding powder
1 large package of instant vanilla pudding powder
2 1/2 cups whole (3%) milk
1/2 cup (125 ml) hazelnut liqueur

Stir until starting to thicken. Pour over Layer 3.

Layer 5:

Spread 2 cups of whipped topping on top of Layer 4. Grate a large milk chocolate bar on top.

How to Host Your Own Sin Supper

Hosting a Sin Supper is great way to connect with friends and loved ones. Put an invitation list together of a group of people who all share something in common. Maybe you have similar jobs, or you all went to the same school. You could all be related, or have lived in the same neighbourhood. Maybe you all worked for the same charity or participated in a project together. Any kind of mutually shared connection will work. It is important to invite people over who already know each other and will be comfortable sharing stories and experiences.

Give your meal a name that starts "Sin Supper with the ...." Make the invitations clear. Everyone brings a dish along with enough copies of the recipe for each person joining the meal. Each dish has to have alcohol in it plus a story to share around it. The more original the recipe is, and the tighter the story and recipe are connected, the better. It's fun if the participants give their recipes names based on the name of the group or theme. Organize the food and have people bring a specific type of dish, such as an appetizer, entrée or dessert to keep the meal balanced.

Give each participant an opportunity to share their story with the group. Meals are usually the best times for sharing. Food is like a glue that holds people together, but as a host, you can decide the best time for the stories to be shared. Make sure each person gets their chance to talk, because in any group there are quiet personalities who may not get heard very well. Remind yourself, along with everyone else, we often think of our lives as ordinary, but each of our lives are actually extraordinary.

Have fun and be flexible with it. It's quite possible the entire group has one story you all shared together. This is a great chance to get together and do something fun to reminisce or reconnect.

Take lots of photos of everyone and the food. Put together a collection of the recipes, stories and photos. Share it with each participant with a scrapbook, on a blog, or on a social media site.

The goal of a Sin Supper is to feed your bodies and your souls and have a little fun along the way.

I would LOVE to hear about your Sin Supper and feature you on the blog! Send me all your information or a link on the submission form at www.CookingWithSin.com.

PALE ALE
666
LAKES

BEER
12 fl. oz.

"Bartender Wannabe" Irish Stew

Irish Stew

I think everyone should go to college and get a degree and then spend six months as a bartender and six months as a cabdriver. Then they would really be educated.
~ Al McGuire

By Heather Pardon

I've never been a one-career kind of gal. In my lifetime, I have worked as a chef, baker, in health promotion, fund raising, events planning and even spent time in a horribly boring office job. I have been a personal chef, worked in a running gear/footwear store, outdoor gear store, been a personal trainer, operated my own bed and breakfast but most of all I enjoy my current position as a Daisymobile driver, author and public speaker.

I enjoy trying new things and there are a few careers I have had on my bucket list of careers to try before I die. One of my career dreams is to work as a bartender. I have spent many years working the back of the house in restaurants as a chef, yet I enjoy getting to know people, and am curious about the bartender's perspective on humanity and the world. And, I also think it would be a blast of fun and likely also make great fodder for a book.

I met some new friends Pamela and Brian who were thinking about opening an Irish Pub. As soon as I caught wind of their plans I was sure to mention my interest in working a few nights a week as a bartender.

One day, Pam called me and asked whether I'd be interested in cooking an Irish dinner for them and a few guests the following Friday. I answered with an enthusiastic "Yes!" I joked with Pam, "Is this my audition for working in the pub?"

I did have to warn both of them that while I'd spent twelve years working as a professional chef, I'd never cooked an Irish stew before. After all, my lineage is Scottish, so I could be forgiven for this. Nonetheless, I accepted the challenge and did some research on traditional Irish pub fare. I eventually came up with this dark stout-laden stew recipe that is an adaptation of a few recipes I came across in my research. I opted to caramelize the vegetables, adding even more colour and flavour to the stew. And serving it with the soda bread is a must!

Ironically, I'd never been able to finish an entire dark stout prior to making this recipe. I put a full can in the stew (add more if you want an even stronger dark stout flavour) and a full can into me during cooking! I think that bodes well for my future career in bartending.

The evening was a huge success. Both the stew and soda bread turned out beautifully. This made me hopeful that one day, even for a short stint, I will be able to take some time away from behind the wheel of my Daisymobile and spend a bit of time behind the bar. In the interim however, I am satisfied that I had one successful evening.

With this stew and a few dark stout on the side, you can re-create your own pub feel right at home with friends. You can be the host, chef and bartender all at once!

Irish Stew

“Bartender Wannabe” Irish Stout Stew

Serves 8

Ingredients:

3 pounds stewing beef, cut into 2” cubes
3 tablespoons oil
2 large onions, coarsely chopped
1 garlic clove, crushed
3 tablespoons all-purpose flour
2 tablespoons tomato paste, dissolved in 4 tablespoons water
1 large can dark stout
2 cups beef stock
Pinch of cayenne
Sprig of fresh thyme
2 cups largely diced carrots
2 cups largely diced parsnip
2 cups largely diced turnip
Salt and freshly ground pepper
Chopped parsley, for garnish

1. Heat 1 tablespoon oil in a large skillet over high heat. Brown the meat on all sides. Do not over crowd the meat while browning. Set aside in a bowl with any pan juices.

2. Reduce the heat, add 1 tablespoon oil to skillet and add the onions and crushed garlic, cooking gently 5 minutes until softened. Add flour and cook mixture together 2 – 3 minutes. Add tomato purée and 1 cup of stout, cover, and cook gently for 5 minutes.

3. Transfer the contents of the skillet and the browned meat to a slow cooker. Pour half of the remaining dark stout into the skillet and bring to a boil. Stir to dissolve any remaining caramelized meat juices from the pan. Pour over the meat, along with the remaining dark stout, beef stock and cayenne. Add the thyme and stir. Cover the slow cooker and cook on high for 1 hour.

4. Heat 1 tablespoon oil in large skillet over medium-high heat. Sauté carrots, parsnips and turnip in batches until brown and slightly caramelized.

5. Add the vegetables to the slow cooker after the meat has cooked for an hour. Stir, cover and continue cooking until meat and vegetables are tender for 1 1/2 – 2 hours. Remove the lid to thicken if needed.

6. Season to taste with salt and pepper before serving and garnish with chopped parsley to serve. It is great with Soda Bread.

Whole Wheat Irish Soda Bread

Ingredients:

2 cups whole-wheat flour
2 cups all-purpose flour, plus more for dusting
1 teaspoon baking soda
1 teaspoon salt
2 1/4 cups buttermilk

1. Preheat oven to 450ºF. Coat a baking sheet with cooking spray and sprinkle with a little flour.

2. Whisk whole-wheat flour, all-purpose flour, baking soda and salt in a large bowl. Make a well in the center and pour in buttermilk. Using one hand, stir in full circles (starting in the center of the bowl working toward the outside of the bowl) until all the flour is incorporated. The dough should be soft but not too wet and sticky. When it all comes together, in a matter of seconds, turn it out onto a well-floured surface. Clean dough off your hand.

3. Pat and roll the dough gently with floury hands, just enough to tidy it up and give it a round shape. Flip over and flatten slightly to about 2 inches. Transfer the loaf to the prepared baking sheet. Mark with a deep cross using a serrated knife and prick each of the four quadrants.

4. Bake the bread for 20 minutes. Reduce oven temperature to 400ºF and continue to bake until the loaf is brown on top and sounds hollow when tapped, 30 to 35 minutes more. Transfer the loaf to a wire rack and let cool for about 30 minutes.

"Canadian Pub" Blackbeard's Chili

Blackbeard's Chi

[Toronto's population is] a mixed race,
neither amalgamated in manners, customs nor habits.
~ Toronto Mayor William Lyon Mackenzie, 1828

An Irishman is the only man in the world who will step over the bodies of a dozen naked women to get to a bottle of stout.
~ Unknown

Taking a job as a cook at an Irish pub in Toronto, Ontario, was a good fit for Mike Crooks. Mike is a Canadian with Irish heritage. His family roots come directly from Ireland. His grandfather, as a young man, immigrated from Ireland to Montreal, Quebec where he raised Mike's father. Then, in the 1970s, Mike's father moved to Oakville, Ontario and that's where Mike grew up.

The pub he was hired to work at was located in the heart of Toronto. It was popular place for university students to hang out.

The owners of the pub were new to the business, and even though Mike had never really cooked before, the owners gave him a lot of latitude. They simply asked him to create the menu for them and trusted him to do so. Mike took a look at some recipe books and started experimenting.

One of the first recipes that caught his eye was called "Blackbeard's Chili." Blackbeard was a fascinating pirate from England who ruled the Atlantic and chili has its origins in Mexico and the southern US. Mike created his own chili dish for the restaurant and used the recipe as his base.

Two of the owners of the Irish pub were from China. The third gentleman was from Pakistan and none of them spoke English very well. Mike was charmed by the fact that he was serving a Mexican dish, named after an English pirate in an Irish pub in Canada that had multi-ethnic owners. It profoundly reflected the multi-cultural Canada we all know and love. He dubbed it the "Canadian Pub."

Mike was surprised recently to find out he may also be part Scottish. His brother came across a Crooks farm settlement in the north of Scotland that had been there for hundreds of years. It is another heritage to add to the mix.

"Canadian Pub" Blackbeard's Chili Con Carne

Serves 10

You will need two pots. One large one for the bulk of the chili (Part I of the recipe) and a second smaller pot for boiling the beans and the beer (Part II of the recipe.)

Part I - The Base Chili Recipe

Ingredients:

900g (2 lbs.) ground beef
2 medium onions, chopped
1 large red bell pepper, chopped
6 cloves garlic, crushed
1 tablespoon fresh oregano leaves
1 tablespoon fresh basil leaves, torn up
1 tablespoon fresh thyme leaves (removed from the stems)
4 tablespoons chili powder
1 1/2 tablespoons cumin powder
1 teaspoon cayenne pepper
2 bay leaves
salt and pepper to taste
1 large can red kidney beans, rinsed
1 large can (796 ml, 28 fl. oz) crushed tomatoes, do not drain
1 5.5 oz. (156 ml) can tomato paste
Shredded cheddar cheese for topping

1. In a large pot, brown the ground beef, making sure to continuously break up large pieces with a spoon or spatula. Once the beef is browned, drain off the fat. Return the ground beef to the pot.

2. Add onions and red bell pepper to the ground beef and cook over medium heat, stirring until the onions are soft and translucent.

3. Add the garlic and stir it while it cooks, for 1 minute, being careful not to let it burn.

4. Add the oregano, basil, thyme, chili powder, cumin, cayenne powder, bay leaves, salt and pepper. Heat over medium heat and stir at regular intervals for 12 minutes.

5. Add the kidney beans, diced tomatoes and tomato paste. Stir to mix well. Reduce heat to low and simmer.

Part II - The Beer and the Beans

Ingredients:

3 cans (19 oz., 540 ml) black beans, rinsed
1 large can dark stout beer

1. Combine the beans and the beer in a medium size pot. Bring to a boil and cook for 30 minutes on medium low.
2. After 30 minutes, remove 1/4 of the beans and set them aside. Cook the rest of the mixture down.
3. Add a little bit of each spice from the chili pot to your simmering pot of beer and beans. It will enhance the flavour of the beer and beans so both pots match better when they are mixed together later on.
4. When the bean and beer mix is thick, remove from heat and purée with a mixer or a food processor.
5. Take the beans you had set aside earlier and add them to your chili. Then take your purée and slowly mix it into your chili. It should add a great texture and amazing flavour to your standard chili recipe.
6. Simmer the combined mixture for 2 hours.
7. Sprinkle shredded cheddar cheese on top of each serving and compliment it with tortilla chips.

"Poverty Line" Yukon Gold German Potato Salad

potato salad

I have a total irreverence for anything connected with society except that which makes the roads safer, the beer stronger, the food cheaper and the old men and old women warmer in the winter and happier in the summer.
~ Brendan Behan

At twenty-four years of age, Ian Szabo was at the peak of his career. After three years of cooking in the finest European restaurants and representing Canada in the Culinary Olympics three times, he was appointed the Executive Sous Chef of one of the top clubs. Running an extremely well organized brigade of over one hundred and twenty people in his kitchen, he served the most distinctive dishes to the city's wealthiest & most influential people. For his own meals, someone from his brigade would bring him the finest foods: lobster, foie gras and fillets of all cuts. Everyday he prepared, served and ate the most exquisite foods in the world.

Then, in a short period of time, everything changed. New management of the club was uncomfortable with Ian's age. They didn't believe he was old enough to handle the responsibilities of his job. Instead of accepting a demotion, he chose to quit. Ian's dad owned a painting company, so he decided to spend some time working with his dad. He knew it would pay some bills and help him fill his day.

One day, during his lunch break, as he sat in the back of the painting van eating his peanut butter sandwich and inhaling the aroma of paint thinner, it struck him that he was now below the poverty line. He had gone from eating the best of the best to living below the poverty line eating the simplest of foods. It was at that moment he decided to start his own business and call it "PLP," "Poverty Line Painting."

Today, seven years later, his business has grown and expanded enormously. Ian appears on television shows, and in newspapers and magazines. He runs a brigade again, but this one works to renovate and upgrade properties. He has taken his brigade system from his kitchen and brought it to his home renovation team and he is happily on top again. No one doubts him now.

Ian still absolutely loves to cook. He finds it very relaxing and fun. One of his favourite meals is a potluck supper with a big twist. He invites friends over and asks each to bring fresh vegetables, meats, fruit or flavours. When everyone arrives, Ian's challenge is to create dishes out of the miscellaneous ingredients. His friends often try to bring obscure ingredients, but I believe he has never been stumped yet!

Modest and delicious food is what Ian prefers to cook. He comes from humble roots and he loves to prepare simple foods in an extraordinary way. Yukon Gold Potato Salad is just one example of this.

Potato Salad

“Poverty Line” Yukon Gold German Potato Salad

Ingredients:

6 large Yukon Gold potatoes, peeled and cut into 1/2 inch cubes
1 tablespoon sea salt
1/2 medium sweet onion, finely diced
2 large shallots, chopped
1 small sprig of thyme, clean off the leaves and discard the stems*
1 small bunch of chives, finely chopped
3 teaspoons Dijon mustard
3 tablespoons herb flavoured vinegar
1/2 cup extra virgin olive oil
1/2 cup German “hefeweizen” wheat beer
Fresh cracked pepper
Sea salt

1. Wash the potatoes, peel them and cook them in water with the sea salt. Cook on medium-high heat for about 20 minutes.

2. Mix the vinaigrette while the potatoes cook. In a large mixing bowl, mix the vinaigrette by adding the shallots, onion, chives, thyme, mustard, olive oil, vinegar and 2 teaspoons of beer. Stir together and add sea salt and pepper to taste.

3. Test the potatoes for firmness. They need to be cooked, but still firm and dense (not soft - like you would for mashing.)

4. Drain the water and add the warm potatoes to the vinaigrette

5. Fold the cubed potatoes and the vinaigrette gently together using a rubber spatula. Cover each potato completely with the vinaigrette, then let it sit for 20 minutes. As it sits, the warmth of the potatoes will warm the vinaigrette and lightly cook the onions and shallots and the potatoes will become infused with the flavours of the vinaigrette.

6. After 20 minutes, test one piece of potato and add flavours to taste. For example, some will prefer it more acidic and add more vinegar, while others will prefer more flavour like pepper or salt.

7. Serve the salad in the large serving bowl that holds the bread plate at the bottom. The juices will go under the bread plate and keep the salad from getting sloppy.

8. Pour the remaining beer in a glass and serve with a wedge of lemon.

*To clean the leaves off a fresh sprig of thyme, lightly grasp it at the base with your finger and thumb. Pull the stem out through your fingers and the leaves will fall off.

"New Life" Home Brew Stew

Home Brew Stew

You can not change your destination overnight,
but you can change your direction overnight.
~ Jim Rohn

Dawn picked up the phone and warmed to Michael's familiar voice, "Dawn Smith, do you love me?"

"Yes. Yes, Michael. I do."

"Good! In thirty minutes a cab will arrive to take you to the airport. I bought your ticket and put $2000 in a bank account for you. You will have to pack quickly. I need you out here with me for my book tour, Dawn."

She hung up the phone and kicked into high gear. The next half hour was a blur of phone calls, packing and panic. A friend offered to take her cat and a neighbour happily took her food. Dawn packed as much as she could and just before the cab pulled up, she called her boss to quit her job.

When she finally sat down in the seat of the cab, Dawn took a deep breath. She was leaving it all behind. It was the right thing to do. She was as ready as she could be for the next phase of her life; eight months on the road with Michael Fletcher and any other adventure that would come their way.

Michael Fletcher and Dawn Smith had known each other for twenty years, but had little contact. They had met briefly as teenagers. Dawn has always been shorter than average and seeing Michael, all 6' 2" tall and full of bravado, she remembers thinking he was the hottest guy she had ever seen. After that, they went their separate ways. They both married other people and started their own businesses. Dawn started a catering company and Michael spent time in the military, followed by several entrepreneurial ventures.

It was New Year's eve, 20 years later. Dawn and Michael were both single again and their paths were about to cross. Dawn's cousin Sandy called her up and invited her to go out to a party. Sandy told her that Michael and a couple of other friends were going to be there, "Dawn, I need your support. You know what these guys are like!" So, Dawn got herself dressed up and out she went.

Dawn remembers vividly the moment she walked into the party. She and Michael locked eyes. They fell in love immediately.

A few days later, Michael had to fly west, back to his home, but their relationship continued. At the time they weren't sure how their long distance relationship would work; they just knew it would work - somehow.

Two months later, the phone call came. Michael was going on a book tour. He knew that Dawn was the best person to have beside him. Their strengths were the perfect compliment. He needed her on this tour and he didn't have the luxury of time.

When Dawn's plane landed, they were off on a whirlwind eight month tour promoting his book. It was a great success. Once the tour wound down, they took the momentum and built up a business that grew even more after they moved back east.

Michael did not want Dawn to lose her identity as a cook, so they agreed to always make a meal together every week. The first night they cooked together, they were watching a chef on television cook a stew. Dawn and Michael both loved the stew so they looked up the recipe online. Using that recipe as a base, they played with it. First, they added their own home brewed beer. Then they added potatoes, parsnips and lots of extra garlic. They also found a recipe for biscuits and did some substituting adding garlic and lots of cheese.

Dawn and Michael have a whole collection of recipes they have created together, and their Home Brew Beer Stew is a favourite at family gatherings. This is the first recipe they created together and the first recipe they have chosen to share with anyone.

"New Life" Home Brew Beef Stew with Garlic Cheese Biscuits

Stew

Ingredients:

1/2 cup vegetable oil
3 lb beef roast, cut into chunks
salt and pepper
1 very large onion, peeled and cut into wedges
8 cloves garlic, peeled and sliced
1 small can tomato paste
2 bottles of Fletcher's Home Brew, or any other lager you choose
2 large potatoes, peeled and cut into chunks
2 parsnips, cut into chunks
2 cups beef stock

1. Preheat oven to 325ºF.

2. Heat oil in very large heavy-bottomed pot suitable for the oven. Add beef, season with salt & pepper and brown the meat.

3. Remove when done and reserve chunks in a bowl.

4. Add onions to the pot and sauté till golden brown. Add garlic and tomato paste and stir together.

5. Add the potatoes, parsnips, beer and return the beef to the pot. Season again with salt and pepper.

6. Cover and place in oven. Stew slowly until beef is tender and broth is thickened, approximately 1 hour.

Home Brew Stew

Garlic Cheese Biscuits

Ingredients:

2 cups flour
1 tablespoon baking powder
1 teaspoon garlic powder
1/2 teaspoon salt
1 cup grated cheddar cheese
1 1/4 cups milk

1. Preheat oven to 450ºF.

2. Whisk together flour, baking powder, garlic and salt.

3. Add cheddar to the flour mix and stir, then add the milk and stir.

4. Turn out onto well-floured board and knead. It will be gooey. Add more flour if necessary.

5. Flatten into a round 1" thick & cut into 8 wedges.

6. Bake on a well-greased baking sheet or pizza stone for 12-15min.

"Would you believe in a love at first sight?
Yes, I'm certain that it happens all the time."
~ John Lennon & Paul McCartney

"Cross Cultural" Chicken Curry

chicken curry

Give me a woman who loves beer and I will conquer the world.
~ Kaiser Wilhelm

Take a Canadian girl, add a Scottish guy, mix with some Chinese flavours and stir in an American beer. What do you get? A great Indian Curry! Really!

Jenni Foss' love of music drew her to concerts and the music industry. In 1997 she uprooted herself from her Canadian home and found a great job at a recording company in London, England. It was at a concert in Camden Town, where she met a handsome and talented Scottish musician named Richard Guy. Richard had been raised in Edinburgh, and was working in London. They fell happily in love and two years later, Richard followed Jenni across the Atlantic, to her home town where they got married.

When Jenni and Richard bought their home, they chose one within walking distance of a good British pub. They wanted to be close to a place with UK beers on tap, authentic pub grub and Indian food.

Marriage requires compromises, and blending two cultures certainly doesn't make it easier. Richard graciously gave up his life in the UK and came to Canada because he loved Jenni dearly. That was never lost on her, and there was one special thing she wanted to do for him.

In Scotland, Richard's favourite comfort food was a curry chicken he liked to order from a local Chinese restaurant. Jenni set out to recreate it for him here in Canada. It turned out to be more challenging than she had anticipated. There are many different kinds of curry and the one Richard had loved back home had been cooked with a British lager. Jenni knew this journey would be as fun as the destination.

Jenni started with a Chinese chicken curry recipe she found in a cookbook. The recipe had the basic ingredients and steps of a good curry and helped her determine the balance of ingredients and flavours. It also used Chinese flavours like soy sauce and toasted sesame oil. As she experimented she adjusted the recipe accordingly. Each attempt was taste-tested with Richard as she tried to get it just right.

The part that stumped Jenni was the beer. She was certain that the restaurant in Scotland had used one of the lagers that are loved throughout the United Kingdom. She tried cooking with all different kinds. On one attempt she tried a strong beer. The next time she tried a heavy beer. She even tried stouts and bitter beers, but none was quite right.

It may have been a moment of desperation or just a lark. One day Jenni added an American lager and that was the ticket! She had not seen that coming. She had finally found the right combination and Richard found some Scottish - well... Scottish-Indian-Chinese - comfort in his new homeland.

"Cross Cultural" Chicken Curry

Serves 4

Ingredients:

2 cups basmati rice
2 tablespoons vegetable oil
3 or 4 boneless, skinless chicken breasts, cut into 1 inch cubes
2 cloves garlic, crushed
2 red peppers, cut into 1 inch pieces
1 block (375 g) paneer cheese cut into 1/2 inch cubes
2 tablespoons madras curry paste
1 tablespoon good quality soy sauce
1/2 bottle American lager
1 teaspoon cornstarch
1/4 cup cold water
2 green onions, finely chopped

1. Wash 2 cups of basmati rice. Then wash it again so it cooks up light and fluffy.

2. Add 3 cups of water and place on high heat and cover. Let boil until pits begin to form in the surface of the rice. Turn off the heat and cover. Let the rice steam while you make the curry.

3. Heat the oil in a stir-fry pan or wok. Add chicken and fry until cooked through, about 4 min. Add the garlic and cook one minute more.

4. Add peppers and paneer to the chicken. Cook, stirring, so the paneer doesn't stick to the bottom of the pan, for 3 minutes or until the peppers begin to soften.

5. Spoon in curry paste and stir until everything in the pan is coated. Add the soy sauce and the beer and stir. Let everything bubble away for a few minutes.

6. Stir the cornstarch into the cold water and pour it into the curry. Let everything come to a boil again so the sauce thickens up.

7. Make a nice cloud of rice in your serving dish. Pour the curry over top. Top with finely chopped green onions. Serve with fresh naan and more beer!

Want to know which beer Jenni prefers in her recipe?
Find out at www.CookingWithSin.com.

Chicken Curry

"Going to the Game" Beer Burgers

Beer Burger

Without question, the greatest invention in the history of mankind is beer. Oh, I grant you that the wheel was also a fine invention, but the wheel does not go nearly as well with pizza.
~ Dave Barry

I find it rather easy to portray a businessman. Being bland, rather cruel and incompetent comes naturally to me.
~ John Cleese

Gary. What can I say? Think of a cross between Clint Eastwood, Steve McQueen, Steven Wright and John Cleese. There is a hidden brilliance there that is surpassed by few. Working in a rather repetitive job in a medium-sized consulting firm, Gary brings a wit and dry humour that keeps his friends laughing and smiling while generally brightening their day.

His friends are called 'Gary's Seedlings'. Most of them are newer to the business and all its facets, but they know a wise, insightful and brilliant comedian when they see one.

You need to understand that Gary has some chronic health concerns that would bring down most anyone. I cannot imagine what strength must be required to keep going with such a weight on his shoulders.

Gary Williams has worked for many people in his life, but he has always marched to the beat of his own drum... or poster... or cane.... or shell collection. A peek at the unique collection of items in his office gives you insight into his sense of humour.

His mind is constantly working, while his body is failing. He never wants any publicity. He would rather spend a few quiet moments in his office than suffer through the inanities of standard office banter. On the other hand, he loves to give a speech in front of a crowd of two hundred and fifty.

Gary has given the annual Christmas speech at the company party for a number of years. Nothing is sacred. With his dry wit and the assistance of a sidekick, he has employees and guests alike laughing till their sides hurt.

If you ask Gary what plans he has for the weekend, he responds dryly, "Stare at the floor and feed my cats." A typical weekend is spent with close friends, having a beer or two, telling stories, and playing a bit of poker.

Gary likes to cook his burgers in beer. He says it's a much healthier way. It was a new concept to me and it's truly delicious.

Recently, Gary was given some negative news about his health from his doctor. When the doctor asked, "What are we going to do now, Gary?" Gary responded, "I am going to the pub to watch the game with my friends."

by Steven Roorda

Beer Burger

Gary's beer cooking technique calls for a great burger recipe to go with it and I found Scooter's "Scooter Pounders."

Scooter is a Youth Worker at an inner city school. He brings his calm and gentle demeanour to the school each day. He is like a kind father figure to the students who hug him and hold on to him physically and emotionally. He is a 6' 4" calm and gentle "oak" in their lives.

I can imagine if Gary and Scooter ever get a chance to meet over a burger and a beer, they will hit it off famously.

Scooter Pounders

Ingredients:

2 lbs. lean beef
2 finely chopped onions
2 teaspoons Worcestershire Sauce
black pepper
1 bunch fresh chopped basil
2 eggs for the binder

Mix all the ingredients together by hand, form into 1/3 pound (150 g) patties.

Scooter likes to barbeque his burgers, but try cooking Gary's beer cooking for something new and really great tasting.

Gary's Beer Cooking Technique

1. Pour 1/2 a bottle of beer in the bottom of a frying pan and place the burgers in the pan. Each patty should be 1/2 or 1/3 immersed in the beer Flip the burgers when you are ready, being careful not to splash the hot beer on yourself.

2. As the beer cooks off, add more of the remaining bottle.

3. Serve with your favourite buns and condiments.

Watch Carla's video where she cooked her own burgers using Gary's beer cooking technique at www.CookingWithSin.com.

"A Suitcase and a Dream" Chocolate Stout Cake

chocolate cake

Aim at Heaven and you will get Earth thrown in.
Aim at Earth and you get neither.
~ C.S. Lewis, Irish-born theologian and author

No matter where you live and what you are surrounded by, if your inner self is not true and authentic, you will feel restless. Sometimes, though, it takes a shift of your physical world to jolt your inner one.

Once after giving the Best Man speech at his close friend's wedding, Philip McKernan got a nudge that a new direction awaited him. Diagnosed with dyslexia as a child, meant that words and writing never came easily to him. He was anxious preparing the speech, so for his own comfort, he decided to be sincere rather than funny. He knew speaking from the heart was the easiest thing to do. He received a standing ovation that day and a stranger in the crowd walked up to him with tears rolling down his face. "I know I have never met you before but if I get married some day would you be my best man? You should speak professionally." It's amazing how a total stranger can make such an impact.

Philip had been raised in an successful business family in Ireland, but sensing a need to break out on his own, Philip made the decision, with his wife Pauline, to leave Ireland and the family business to start a new venture in Canada. When he landed on Canadian soil, he looked at his suitcase and thought, "I'm here with a suitcase in my hand and a dream in my heart. I am ready for whatever lies ahead."

Philip's new business grew quickly and he began mentoring new start-ups. People began asking him to speak and before long he had speaking engagements across the country. Over time, he noticed a recurring theme. While many people were happy with their businesses, he met too many who were miserable. They had given so much to their businesses that their families were torn apart or they were suffering physically. Busy doing what seemed to be important, they hadn't stop to ask whether it supported their true passions and they had become lost.

Philip recognized the same struggle within himself, so he took some time to reflect. He really saw how many of his personal decisions had been influenced by external forces in his life. He realized that he, and the people he was mentoring, would only find peace of mind when they followed a path that was authentic to themselves alone.

Philip left Ireland with a plan to build an new business across the Atlantic. His dyslexia had always been a significant obstacle, so he never imagined he would become an international speaker and write two books - with more in the works. Philip found his real genuine purpose was beyond his business plans. The true dream in his heart as he held his suitcase at the airport, was to speak, write and coach to help other people find their own true authentic purpose.

Philip enjoys drinking a good Irish stout and Pauline enjoys baking. Putting the two together creates this wonderful cake and it gives them a wee taste of life back home in Ireland.

"Getting to a point in life that you can be truly proud of yourself
is a STUNNING place to be. Let's be stunning!
~ Philip McKernan

"A Suitcase and a Dream" Chocolate Stout Cake

Ingredients:

1 cup dark stout beer
1/2 cup unsalted butter (cut into pieces)
3/4 cup cocoa
2 rounded cups caster sugar (fine white sugar)
3/4 cup sour cream
2 eggs
1 tablespoon real vanilla extract
2 cups all-purpose flour
2 1/2 teaspoons baking soda

1. Preheat oven to 350ºF.

2. Butter a 9 inch spring form pan and line the bottom and the corners with parchment. Lightly dust the sides with cocoa powder.

3. Place beer in a large saucepan and add the butter. Heat on medium heat until the butter melts, then whisk in the cocoa and sugar.

4. In a bowl beat together the sour cream, eggs and vanilla and then pour into the beer mixture, then whisk in the flour and soda.

5. Pour into the cake pan, cook for 45 minutes to an hour, remove from oven, place on a cooling rack and leave to cool in the pan.

Topping Ingredients:

8 oz. cream cheese
1 1/4 cups icing sugar
1/2 cup whipping cream

1. Whip the cream cheese until smooth. Sift in the icing sugar and beat together.

3. Add the cream and beat together again for several minutes until it is smooth, spreadable and frothy.

4. Place cooled cake on a flat serving dish, spread the topping on the top only. The cake will resemble a beautiful pint of creamy stout!

Find out more about Philip's personal journey at www.CookingWithSin.com.

Beer Aroma Wheel

by Courtesy of Annette Schmelzle • www.beeraromawheel.com

Aroma wheels provide a terminology for the sensory description of products. They were developed to help people responsible for quality control and product development to communicate using unambiguous terminology. 30 years ago, Meilgaard developed the beer flavour wheel. Its development was an important milestone in establishing an accepted terminology for the sensory science of beer. It still serves as the basis for the selection of terms in descriptive profiling tests today.

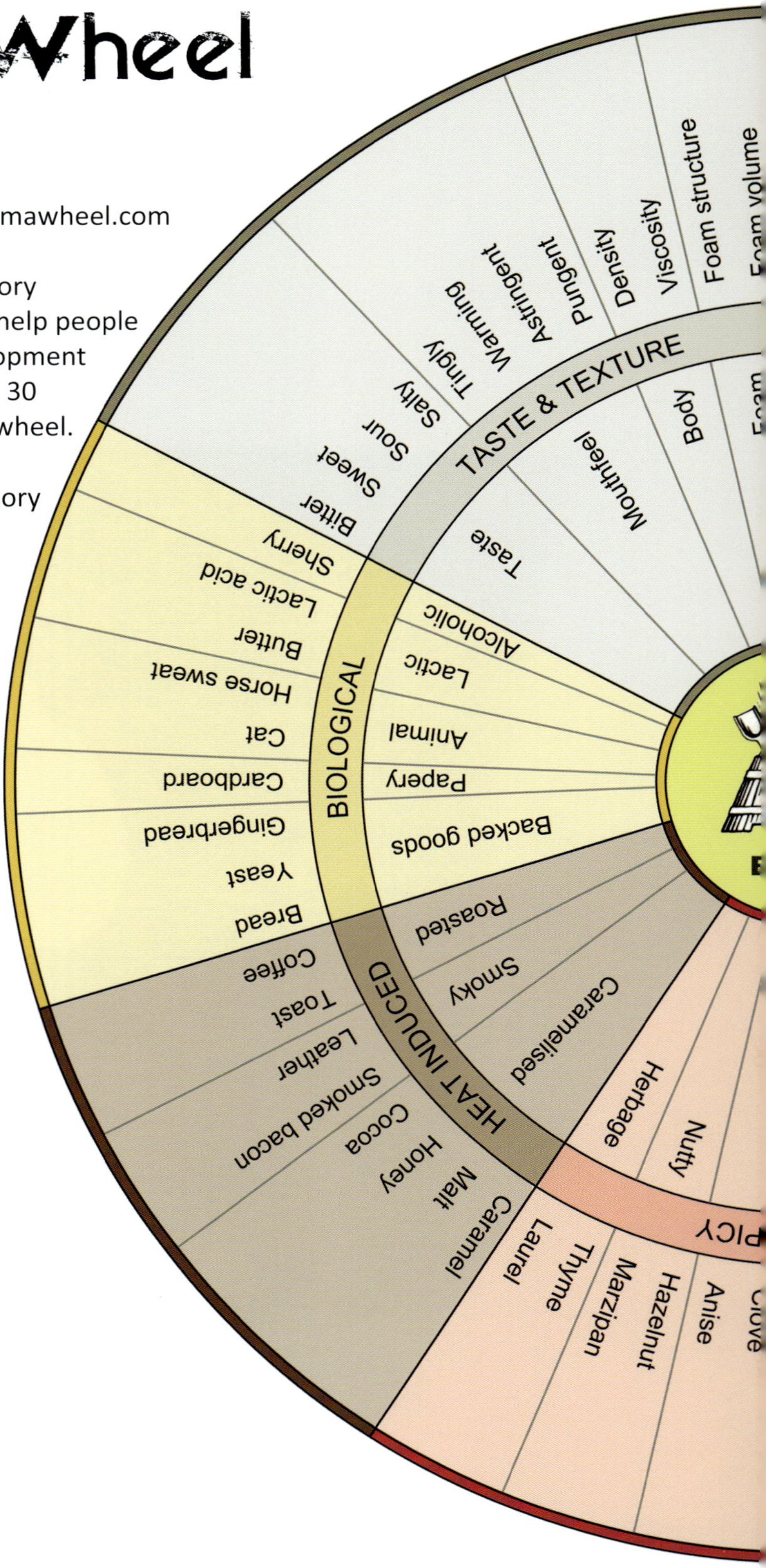

Aroma Wheel

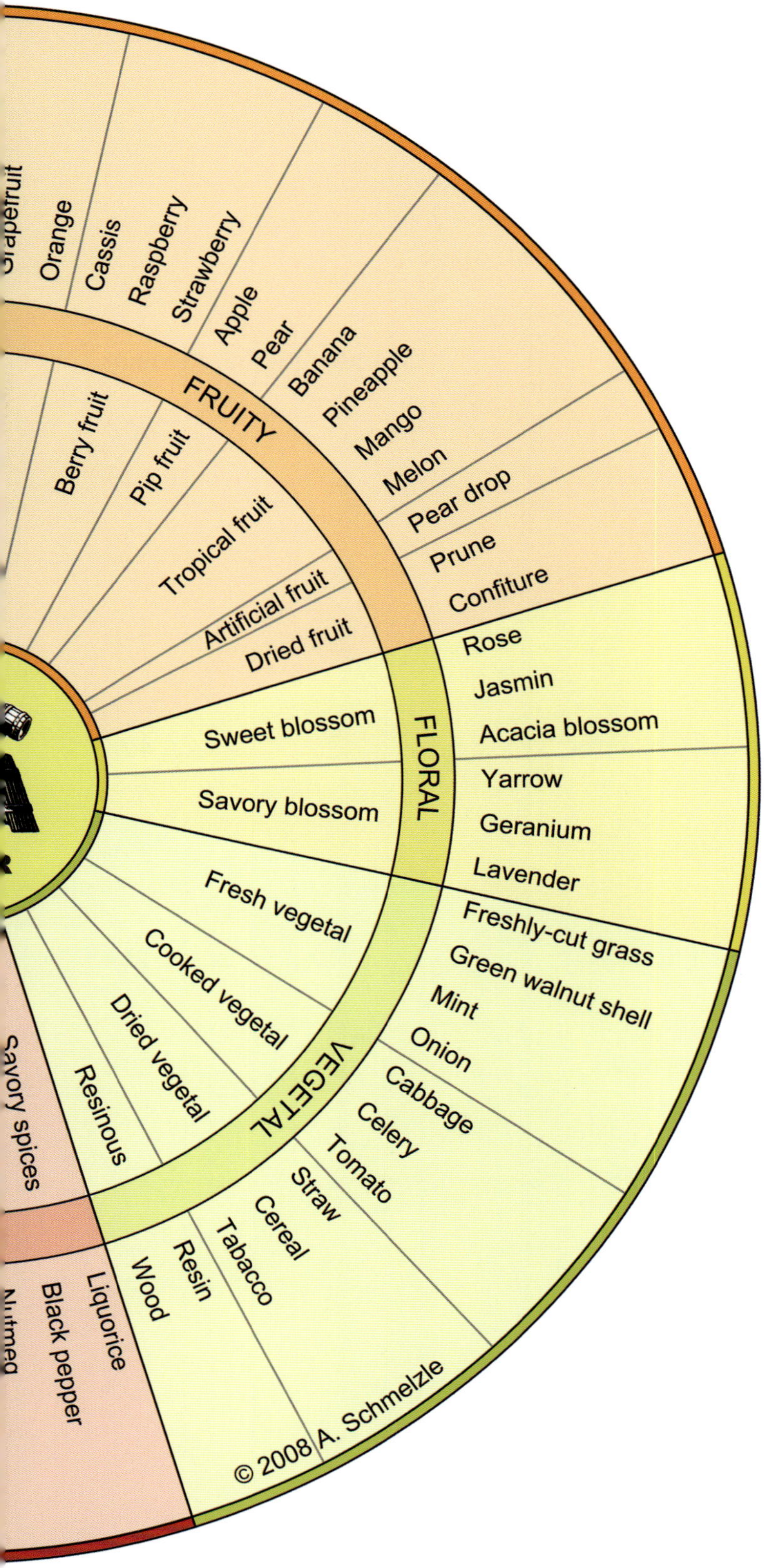
FRUITY
Berry fruit
Pip fruit
Tropical fruit
Artificial fruit
Dried fruit
Grapefruit
Orange
Cassis
Raspberry
Strawberry
Apple
Pear
Banana
Pineapple
Mango
Melon
Pear drop
Prune
Confiture
FLORAL
Sweet blossom
Savory blossom
Rose
Jasmin
Acacia blossom
Yarrow
Geranium
Lavender
VEGETAL
Fresh vegetal
Cooked vegetal
Dried vegetal
Resinous
Freshly-cut grass
Green walnut shell
Mint
Onion
Cabbage
Celery
Tomato
Straw
Cereal
Tabacco
Resin
Wood
Savory spices
Liquorice
Black pepper
© 2008 A. Schmelzle

WHEN IS IT NO LONGER "SIN" FUL

Alcohol Burn-Off Chart

How much alcohol remains in the food when it is cooked? The answers may surprise you. The following chart shows different cooking methods, various cooking times and the percentage of alcohol that remains afterwards.

Preparation: Alcohol is: **% of Alcohol that Remains**

- Added but no heat is used and the food is stored overnight 70%
  Example: "Special Delivery" Black Forest Cake

- Stirred into a hot liquid and served immediately 85%
  Example: "Savoury Scent" Chicken Soup

- Flambéed 75%
  Example: "She's a Trooper" Cherries Jubilee

- Stirred into the food and it is baked or simmered for 15 minutes 40%
  Example: "Roman Holiday" Spaghetti Carbonara

- Stirred into the food and it is baked or simmered for 30 minutes 35%
  Example: "Sin Supper" Pasta de la Coeur

- Stirred into the food and it is baked or simmered for 1 hour 25%
  Example: "Comfort of Home" Sherry Potatoes

- Stirred into the food and it is baked or simmered for 1.5 hours 20%
  Example: "Ci Vediamo" Spezzatino

- Stirred into the food and it is baked or simmered for 2 hours 10%
  Example: "Just like Gold" Jamaican Rum Cake

- Stirred into the food and it is baked or simmered for 2.5 hours 5%
  Example: "Bartender Wannabe" Irish Stew

- Added but not stirred in and the food is baked or simmered for 25 minutes 45%
  Example: "We Are Family" Whisky Brie

USDA Table of Nutrient Retention Factors, Release 6, December 2007
http://www.ars.usda.gov/nutrientdata

Burn-Off

PARTICIPANT CONTACT INFORMATION

Here is the contact information for some of the participants, in alphabetical order, according to their surnames. I know each of them would be very happy to get to know you.

Campbell, Bob & Margaret • www.ColourTech.com
Chef D (Darryl Fletcher) • www.ChefDTV.com
Chef Janet • www.SatisfiedSoul.com
Chef Suman • www.ChefSuman.com
Chef Tim Wasylko • www.TimWasylko.com
Fletcher, Michael • www.neworldcoaching.com
Johnson, Michelle • www.MichelleJohnson.ca
Jurczyk, Heather • www.HeCooksSheCooks.com
Kleim, Heather • Epic Empire Designs Home Staging • www.EpicEmpireDesigns.ca
McKernan, Philip & Pauline • www.PhilipMckernan.tv
Pardon, Heather • www.WildDaisy.ca
Runciman, Darcelle • www.DarcelleRunciman.com
Shively, Jeff • www.HeCooksSheCooks.com
Smith, Dawn • www.NeworldCoaching.com
Stone, Shelley • www.OntarioGleaners.org
Szabo, Ian • www.PLPContracting.com

MORE PHOTO CREDITS

Page 12 photo of Carla: Daren Roorda
Page 33 photo of Barry & Tara: Hannah Carter www.redumbrellaphotography.ca
Page 37 photo of Heather: Jessi Connaughton.
Page 43 photo of family: Katy Hersey http://picturemefoto.wordpress.com
Page 51 photo of Roasted Rabbit : Andriy Zolotoiy
Page 83 photo of statue: H.T. Lam & wedding photo: Joshua Lam
Page 95 & 97 photos of Chef Janet: Donna Kearns
Page 111 headshot of Darcelle: Rose-anne Turunen www.reallifechanges.com
Page 143 photos of wedding: Darren Rigo
Page 149 photo of family: Tamara L.
Page 181 headshot: Perry Thompson & coffee shop photo: Jourdain Gadoury
Page 189 photo of Mike: Sarah Mills
Page 217 "Testing the Atlantic": Gary Williams & "Shell Collection": Steven Roorda
Page 223 photo of family: Myshsael Schlyecher www.myshsael.com
Back cover headshot of Carla: Kim Nielsen www.kimnielsenphotography.ca

INDEX

We're Toast!